Physical Characteristics of the German Shorthaired Pointer

(from the American Kennel Club breed standard)

Back: Short, strong, and straight with a slight rise from the root of the tail to the withers. The loin is strong, is of moderate length, and is slightly arched.

Tail: Set high and firm, and must be docked, leaving approximately 40% of its length.

Hindquarters: Thighs are strong and well muscled. Stifles are well bent. Hock joints are well angulated and strong with straight bone structure from hock to pad.

Color: May be of solid liver or a combination of liver and white such as liver and white ticked, liver patched and white ticked, or liver roan.

Coat: Hair is short and thick and feels tough to the hand.

Size: Height of dogs, measured at the withers, 23 to 25 inches. Height of bitches, measured at the withers, 21 to 23 inches. Weight of dogs 55 to 70 pounds. Weight of bitches 45 to 60 pounds.

Feet: Compact, close-knit and round to spoon-shaped. The toes are sufficiently arched and heavily nailed. The pads are strong, hard and thick.

German Shorthaired Pointer

◇

By Nona Kilgore Bauer

Contents

KENNEL CLUB BOOKS® GERMAN SHORTHAIRED POINTER
ISBN: 1-59378-274-8

Copyright © 2003, 2006 • Kennel Club Books LLC
308 Main Street, Allenhurst, NJ 07711 USA
Cover Design Patented: US 6,435,559 B2 • Printed in South Korea

10 9 8 7 6 5 4 3 2

PHOTO CREDITS:
Norvia Behling, Mary Bloom, T. J. Calhoun, Carolina Biological Supply, Doskocil, Isabelle Français, James Hayden-Yoav, James R. Hayden, RBP, Bill Jonas, Dwight R. Kuhn, Dr. Dennis Kunkel, Mikki Pet Products, Phototake, Jean Claude Revy, Dr. Andrew Spielman and Alice van Kempen.

Illustrations by Renée Low.

Showing off his natural versatility as a hunter, this German Shorthaired Pointer is posing with his fluffy retrieve.

GERMAN SHORTHAIRED POINTER

Born to run...born to reign. In a sporting world dominated by several breeds of utility gundog that are proficient in hunt, point and retrieve (HPR), the German Shorthaired Pointer (GSP) stands alone as the premier hunting dog of Europe and the revered national gundog of Germany. Possessed of that indefinable ability to run unerringly on a scent in all types of cover and terrain, then, upon finding the game, slow into a feline crouch and freeze, sculpture-like into stone, the GSP is universally regarded as the near-perfect all-around gundog.

The GSP, like other gundog breeds that evolved during the 19th century, developed when hunting finally became a sport of the common man. For centuries, birds and animals were hunted for both food and sport. The aristocrat pursued small and large game for personal entertainment and challenge, while the ordinary man did so to feed his family and himself. To that end, the scenthound tracked partridge and other game birds, while the

HUNTING WITH BIRDS
In many parts of Europe and the Middle East, falcons, eagles and hawks are still used in tandem with dogs in the hunting sport. The dog points and holds the birds, and the falcon is released to circle overhead and wait, swooping down once the birds are flushed. Falconry, however, is against the law in certain countries.

hunter followed with netting to throw and snare the birds. The dogs and nets were sometimes used in tandem with a hawk or falcon, which would then capture the birds in flight as they attempted to escape.

The introduction of the shotgun in the 1800s changed the nature of the hunt for both man and beast. At that time, European aristocracy owned and bred a wide variety of dogs, each type specializing in a different aspect of the hunt, to accompany them on their shoots. Pointers and setters raced ahead of the hunting party, located the game and stood fast. Retrievers followed and "picked up" game after it was shot. The spaniel breeds worked closely with the hunter, flushing as well as retrieving.

The average citizen could not afford to keep large kennels of highly specialized breeds to perform all of the tasks necessary for a successful hunt; that is,

separate breeds to point, to flush and to retrieve shot game. Thus was born a myriad of efforts across Europe to produce a truly versatile hunting dog: one breed to perform all of these tasks.

The practical German hunter-breeder aimed for the ideal one-man dog, one with a superb nose that could locate, point and hold until the guns were at the ready, then, with a gentle mouth, retrieve the bird to hand. Such a dog should also possess great courage and the ability and willingness to stalk and apprehend larger game such as deer, hare or fox. The hunter also demanded a dog with a sound temperament that could bond to his family when not working in the field. These hunters did not want kennels full of dogs for various purposes; in fact, they did not want kennels full of dogs at all. Rather, they aimed for one dog skilled in all of the hunting tasks that they could keep in their homes as family companions.

The two dogs used most commonly to achieve those breeding goals shared the same ancestry as many other European dogs, most being descendants of the St. Hubert Hound and the Old Spanish Pointer, two ancient Mediterranean breeds that reached Europe along with civilization.

Allegedly brought there by the Knights of the Crusaders

STALKING DEER
German Shorthaired Pointers are still used for stalking deer in many countries. The hunter hangs a wooden baton on a loose rope around the dog's neck and sends his dog off to find a wounded deer that has been shot. Upon finding the deer, the dog returns to his master, holding the baton in his mouth, and the hunter follows the dog to where his quarry lies. If the dog is unsuccessful, he will come back with the baton still hanging from his neck.

during the 11th century, the Hounds of St. Hubert can be traced directly back to the famed French monastery. A descendant of the courageous eighth-century staghound, the St. Hubert is the ancestor of all cold-trailing hounds. Like the Old Spanish Pointer, these black hounds were also known in Germany as *Schweisshunden*, expert cold trailers who possessed exquisite noses and hunted with great persistence. Historic documents and artwork describe the Old Spanish Pointer as a heavy-headed, jowly animal with drooping flews, large bone structure, a slightly rough liver-and-white coat and an often surly attitude. Both breeds were ponderous and slow-moving, hardly worthy qualities to complement the use of firearms on the hunting scene. But the

scenting and pointing abilities of both breeds were so superb that both aristocrat and common man set out to add elegance and speed in the hope of reaching their vision of a more versatile pointing dog.

By the late 1800s, Germany, France and England were well into their own pointer breeding programs. The early Germans used the black type to fix one version of the German Short-haired Pointer. By the mid-1900s, the Scandinavian countries still had some solid blacks; in Australia, that country's best-known pointer breeder also had

With the GSP's regal, intelligent expression, it's no wonder that royalty was attracted to the breed.

experimental dog bred by Prince
Albrecht zu Solms-Brauenfels of
the Royal House of Hannover.
Feldmann I was a ponderous-
looking, short-legged dog with
the traditional heavy head and
thicker neck, hardly a prime
example of the swift and graceful
animal for which breeders
strived.

Breeding efforts continued
throughout Europe and, in
Germany, a wide variety of breed
types emerged. Proponents of the
breeding principle that "function
follows form" believed a dog's
physical construction was
primary and that natural ability
would eventually follow. They
pursued a pointing dog that
possessed rounded ears and a
classic profile (with no stop), a
preference that was held mostly
in rebellion against the English
Pointer's small, tight ears and
dish-faced head. In their quest
for their desired head type, these
advocates inevitably produced
heavy-bodied, short-legged,
awkward dogs that were unable
to fulfill the German vision of
speed and elegance in the field.

a solid black bitch in her
program. The United States also
had solid liver colors, as demon-
strated in one historic painting
that hangs in the De Young
Museum in San Francisco. All of
the countries appeared to strive
for wrinkle-free heads with
straighter profiles, rounded ears
and more leg under the dog.

By the late 1900s, Europe
saw mixed results in the effort to
produce good-looking, properly
balanced pointing dogs. The
French promoted the Gascon
Hound, Genereaux, their prize-
winning hound at the 1865 Paris
Exhibition. Genereaux was a
long-tailed, wrinkle-free sporting
dog that easily reminds one of
the German Shorthaired Pointer
seen today. Germany's 1871
showing, however, was the
ungainly Feldmann I, a tricolor

The breeders who believed in
"function follows form," led by
German breeder Karl Brandt, in
1879 convinced the committee to
deny Stud Book admission to
any pointer who did not carry
the desired characteristics, a
move that subsequently denied
admission to many deserving

specimens of the breed.

Into that foray came the highly respected Prince zu Solms-Brauenfels. Having gained valuable experience in his earlier experimental breedings, especially with Feldmann I, the Prince advocated the opposite principle, that of "form follows function." Like other wise pioneer breeders, the Prince looked primarily at performance and bred selectively to produce the best performers, using dogs of various type, different breeds and different strains of breeds, believing that once performance was firmly established, one could later select for structure.

The Prince advised the German breeders to use only the best performing dogs for breeding stock. At his direction, many adjusted their breeding decisions and looked solely to ability, with some forward-thinkers, outlaws in German breeding terms, using the English Pointer to enhance the already splendid quality of nose and pointing instinct.

With English Pointer blood, however, came one more element of risk. The cross eventually reduced trailing ability, diminished enthusiasm for the water and diluted courage in pursuit of larger game.

Nevertheless, the determined efforts of the breeders seeking function first produced one of the early solid working German

Shorthaired Pointers, named Nero 66 (66 being his number in the Kurzhaar Stud Book), bred by Herr Julius Mehlich. A brown chest-ticked dog with a good nose and showing excellent strength and speed, Nero

INSTINCTIVE ABILITY
The ability to seek scent to locate game, then to stand rigid at the finding has been bred into the German Shorthaired Pointer for many generations and is a skill that cannot be taught. The dog can be trained to best utilize that natural ability, but the talent is born with the dog.

performed well at the 1881 pointer/setter trial at Buckow. The pointer world again took note of Nero when, two years later, he tied with another brown pointer named Treff 1010 (his all-breed registration number) for first place in the German Derby.

Following his Derby achievement, Nero and his owner were invited to join a hunting party at the famed Hoppenrade hunting

TICKING

The ticking on the German Shorthaired Pointer's coat will appear almost white at birth. Ticking starts to appear between two and three weeks of age.

preserve owned by an aristocrat named Herr Schmidt. On that occasion, it was Nero's famous escapade with a hare that gave birth to the renowned Hoppenrade strain of German Shorthaired Pointers. During the hunt, Nero sped off after a shot hare and was gone so long that the anxious hunting party thought the dog might have been injured somewhere afield. To their delight, Nero finally appeared on the far bank of a fast-running stream, the huge hare clamped firmly in his jaws. The dog then plunged into the racing river waters and fought his way across to deliver his catch to his master. Herr Schmidt applauded the dog's valiant effort and proudly announced to the jubilant onlookers, "From this time on, you are no longer Nero 66; you are Nero v. Hoppenrade! And the name shall be given to all your descendants as well."

Thus was born the distinguished line of Hoppenrade German Shorthaired Pointers, whose names can be found behind most modern GSP pedigrees. It is most fitting that Nero's granddaughter, Erra Hoppenrade 382, earned the number-one spot in the *Gebrauchshunde-Stammbuch* (German Working Dog Stud Book) after she beat the competition in 1892.

Other Hoppenrade offspring

Although not a water retriever by trade, the GSP is certainly versatile enough to be trained for the task or just to enjoy an occasional swim.

followed in Nero's famous pawprints, placing in many Derby stakes. Nero's daughter Flora later produced three influential solid-brown dogs when she was bred to Hektor 64 (Treff ex Diana): two males (Waldin 175, Waldo 174) and the female Hertha. Waldin continued his famous grandsire's legacy with an impressive performance of his own at a pointer/setter field trial at Buckow. At that trial, the German Emperor was so taken with Waldin's work that he commissioned the dog's portrait to be painted by the renowned German artist Sperling.

Other Hoppenrade dogs can be found in a great many foundation breed pedigrees. Herr Mehlich's bitch Holla (Hoppenrade) was the first full-ticked specimen in his line of solid

GERMAN CHAMPIONSHIP

The German title *Sieger* denotes a champion, with *Siegerin* for the female champion. To achieve that title, a dog must earn three first prizes with a rating of *Vorsuglich* (Excellent) under three different approved judges at approved shows. It must qualify in performance as well as conformation.

The *Kurzhaar Sieger* must earn first prizes in the Derby and the Solms, and second place or better in a Klub Utility Search (*Verbandsgebrauchsprufung*), or Derby or Solms first place plus first place in the Klub Utility Search. The dog must also qualify by running well in the Kleeman Search, and later qualify on the trail (*Verlorenbringenprufung*) of a wounded hare (*krankgeschossenen Hasen*) that the dog has not previously seen. Excellence in all events proves that the dog is capable in all aspects of natural working ability.

brown, chest-ticked dogs. Holla produced sons Morell 444 (Holla ex Waldin 175) and Maitrank (Holla ex Balsam Hoppenrade), who later became foundation dogs in many pedigrees.

The dog Treff 1010 also provides another stepping stone in German Shorthaired Pointer history. The breedings of Nero offspring to Treff sons and grand-children form the foundation of most pedigrees of the breed.

When discussing German Shorthaired Pointer history and pedigrees, one cannot ignore the age-old debate over the presence of the Bloodhound in the breed's development. Despite the over-whelming evidence that GSP ancestry goes back to the Old Spanish Pointer and variations of the Hounds of St. Hubert, argu-ments still persist that Blood-hound crosses figure into the formation of the breed. Although that notion is still accepted by some English breed historians, knowledgeable German authori-ties have adamantly rejected the Bloodhound theory many times.

One reason for the Blood-hound misconception may lie in the fact that in the German language, *schweiss* means "scent...and blood trail...as in hunting." *Hund* means dog, thus any dog who follows a trail is a *Schweisshund*, though not neces-sarily a Bloodhound. So while the German name for the Blood-hound is Schweisshund, it is also a term often used to describe the early working German Shorthaired Pointer. One truth does lie in the fact that the Bloodhound shares an ancestor with the German Shorthaired Pointer, with both breeds, along with many others, tracing back to the Hounds of St. Hubert.

An undisputed fact is that throughout 19th-century Europe, every country was attempting to shape its own desired version of the ideal scenthound. Fortu-nately, any mention of a Blood-hound cross with the German Shorthaired Pointer has been removed from recent books that chart the development of the breed. Older versions still exist, however, available to the unsus-pecting novice who may inno-cently accept the Bloodhound theory as fact.

The unification of Germany as a

AIR SCENTING
The German Shorthaired Pointer seeks game by air scenting, running with his head high to take efficient advantage of the wind. He does not "ground" or "foot" scent, which is following the scent left on the ground by running game. He will, however, follow a "foot" or "blood" scent to trail a wounded bird.

There is a debate over whether or not the well-known Bloodhound is among the GSP's forefathers.

sovereign nation in 1870 gave the breeding community the cohesion necessary to raise their efforts to a national level. In 1891, breed fanciers founded the *Klub Kurzhaar* (Shorthair Club), a reorganization of the previous *Brantiger Klub*. Today about 25 regional German Shorthaired Pointer breed clubs operate throughout Germany under the umbrella of the parent organization *Deutsch Kurzhaar Verband*.

As with other breeds, breed progress and development were seriously interrupted by World War II (1939 to 1945). Recovery was even more difficult for the German effort, due to the division of the German nation into East and West Germany. Still the German Shorthaired Pointer has persevered, standing without equal, a handsome utility dog capable of excellence in all aspects of the hunt, whether in field, wood or water.

THE BREED IN THE US

The GSP arrived in America around 1925 when a one-year-old bitch named Senta v. Hohen-bruck, bred by Herr Edwardt Reindt (Hohenbruck strain) of Austria, was imported by Dr. Charles Thornton of Montana. Senta was in whelp when she arrived in the United States, and she produced the first seven GSPs born here. Six survived, named Frisky, Smarty, Pep,

Queen, King and Bob, and they represented the range of GSP colors: ticked, solid brown and brown and white. Dr. Thornton became a true advocate of the breed, and he established his kennels over the next five years with imports from many other great German strains. Although far too many of Dr. Thornton's litters went to hunters who didn't bother to register their dogs or who outcrossed them in indiscriminate breedings, a practice that greatly distressed Thornton, many of his dogs went on to establish the first GSP stronghold in the American pure-bred dog community. The term "Thornton breeding" is often used to describe the foundation of the breed in the United States.

American hunters accepted the breed enthusiastically. The American Kennel Club (AKC) gave the GSP formal recognition in March 1930, with the registration of German import Greif v. d. Fliegerhalde, whelped in 1928. The first AKC-licensed specialty show was held in March 1941 as part of the International Kennel Club show.

It was not until 15 years after the breed's AKC recognition that the German Shorthaired Pointer Club of America (GSPCA), today the breed's national parent club, was formed. Before then, in 1939, the Minnesota German

American hunters enthusiastically welcomed the German Shorthaired Pointer to their shores. The breed was used widely for a variety of game on the massive land stretches of the US.

Shorthaired Pointer Club func-
tioned as the breed's parent club
in the US, and it remained so
until 1953. It was about a decade
later before the GSPCA was reor-
ganized into the structure under
which it functions today.

One interesting dispute
continues in the US over the
matter of breed name recognition. By the time the AKC recognized the breed in 1930, calling
it the German Shorthaired
Pointer, the German Club had
already trimmed "Pointer" from
its name, making it now the
German Shorthair. The name
change by German breed devel-
opers was effected in order to
remove the dog from the Pointer
class. They also hoped to
prevent any more infusion of
Pointer blood, the cross used to
increase speed in large running
dogs.

In the US, the GSP is generally considered no match in All-
Age Field Trials when pitted
against the pointer breeds with
which he must compete. The
breed has many dual champions,
dogs that have earned their titles
both in the show ring and in the
field.

Since the German Short-
haired Pointer's introduction to
the US and acceptance by the
AKC, it has become one of our
country's most popular Sporting
breeds. He earned his sparkling
reputation in America by prov-

ing his ability as a hunter and as
a family companion reliably over
the years, and he is as wonderful
in the home as he is in the field.
For a dog with so many skills, he
also is a loving and playful dog
in the home, a favorite with children and always loyal to his
family.

THE BREED IN BRITAIN

Prior to World War II, British
sportsmen and wealthy landown-
ers used specialist breeds on
their hunting ventures—the swift
game-finding pointers on the
moors, the retrievers for picking
up and the spaniels for rough
shooting. Little was known of the
all-purpose utility dogs that
performed the tasks of all those
breeds combined. In the post-war
years, when large estates were
sold and later divided, the
nature of shooting changed, with
more commoners taking up the
sport on smaller pieces of
ground, an ideal scenario for an
all-purpose dog like the German
Shorthaired Pointer.

Although breed historians
note that specimens of the breed
were observed and documented
in England prior to the war
years, in fact as early as 1887,
the breed more notably arrived
in the country during the late
1940s as hunting companions of
British army officers who discovered the breed while on hunting
forays when they were stationed

in Germany. Although these dogs undoubtedly became the foundation of the breed in Britain, anti-German sentiment was strong and anything bearing a Teutonic influence was not readily accepted. Given local prejudice and a very limited gene pool, breed advancement during the last half of the 20th century was slow when compared to that of the spaniel and retriever breeds, most of which originated in Britain.

By the mid-1990s, about 10,000 GSPs had been registered with England's Kennel Club. While few of these are exhibited in field events or the show ring, the great majority exist as prized hunting companions of their hunter-owners. This lack of diversity has also helped to set type, with little difference observed between the hunting GSP and those in the show ring, a position envied by other breeds that have suffered the vagaries of popularity.

The German Shorthaired Pointer Club in England was founded in 1851 at the direction of Geoffrey Sterne, later club president, with goals to establish field trials and championship status for the breed. Some 20 years later, the German Shorthaired Pointer Association was formed, providing more opportunity for field trials, shows and inter-club competition. Each

The German Shorthaired Pointer is a steady and friendly dog, able to adapt to most any situation.

organization carries 600 to 800 members, many of whom belong to both clubs.

A third supporting group, the Field Trial Association for Hunt, Point and Retrieve, works as a bonding agent for all HPR breed societies. With a membership base of two representatives from each HPR organization, the group forms an umbrella society to keep associated clubs advised on field-trial matters, provide a forum for field-trial considerations and represent the field-trial groups to The Kennel Club. They also conduct judges' seminars and organize the annual Championship Stake for The Kennel Club.

Characteristics of the
GERMAN SHORTHAIRED POINTER

GSPs have a natural affinity for children, as well as for "people" food. It is wise to monitor your GSP's relationship with both.

The German Shorthaired Pointer is, first and foremost, a versatile and athletic gundog, bred to work long days in the field. He is a most suitable companion for the foot hunter who enjoys an all-around dog with which to hunt and a pleasant companion with which to live. He can also serve as a most agreeable family companion for the non-hunter who is willing to accommodate the breed's boundless energy. The GSP is not a suitable pet for people who cannot provide vigorous exercise and mental stimulation as well as a moderate degree of training and discipline. The ideal family for a GSP would be active and outgoing people who enjoy outdoor activities.

This is a most friendly and intelligent dog with a naturally happy disposition. He is loyal and protective and gets along well with children, although early socialization with them is most important. Indeed, he will bond well with all members of the family but is generally reserved with strangers. He is quite people-oriented, with a strong desire to please. He can become devoted to

GSPs require significant daily exercise. Running free in a secured area is an excellent way to exercise your dog. Retrieving objects takes advantage of your GSP's "birdy" instincts.

the point of dependency and would not thrive if he were isolated from his human family.

Although he enjoys living within the family unit, his high energy level demands that he be well exercised at least twice a day to satisfy his activity needs and prevent boredom from taking hold. A bored GSP, deprived of human companionship or exercise, can become agitated and destructive.

Although the GSP is considered a medium-sized dog, he is not a good prospect for living in an apartment and does best in a house with a large yard. The yard or play area should be enclosed by at least a 6-foot-high fence, as this is a talented escape artist who can

easily scale a fence, especially if he is bored or underexercised. Free running in an open area is never encouraged as an exercise option, a principle that applies to all dogs, regardless of breed. Of course, your GSP's favorite kind of exercise will be that shared with his owner!

The male GSP tends to be more dominant and outgoing, and is a more aggressive hunter. He will also require a more dominant owner or handler who can sustain the position of superior to the dog. The female GSP is more submissive and less inclined to dominance. The energy level of a GSP of either sex may vary, depending on the pedigree and breeding.

Dogs bred for high performance in the field will require greater activity than those bred for conformation or as family companions.

German Shorthaired Pointers will get along well with other dogs and cats if they are raised with them or socialized with them during puppyhood. If not conditioned to other animals in their youth, they may view smaller animals as prey and become a threat to them, stalking any strange cats or passing squirrels. As a breed, they are considered barkers, so do not encourage your pup to bark from the onset and consider teaching a "quiet" command so that you can discourage excessive barking.

DOGS, DOGS, GOOD FOR YOUR HEART!

People usually purchase dogs for companionship, but studies show that dogs can help to improve their owners' health and level of activity, as well as lower a human's risk of coronary heart disease. Without even realizing it, when a person puts time into exercising, grooming and feeding a dog, he also puts more time into his own personal health care. Dog owners establish more routine schedules for their dogs to follow, which can have positive effects on their own health. Dogs also teach us patience, offer unconditional love and provide the joy of having a furry friend to pet!

TRAINING FOR THE FIELD

There are many methods of training a German Shorthaired Pointer for field work. Although the GSP is, or should be, a proficient gundog, his skills must be honed if he is to be an efficient and compatible hunting companion. Basic obedience is an essential part of owning any dog and must be taught by the owner or handler. This will not in any way diminish the dog's desire to work at his inherited instincts, but rather will enhance the opportunity to discover his inherent capabilities.

Commands such as "Sit" and "Stay," walking at heel, steadiness to shot, recalling from a distance and retrieving are most important lessons in the hunting dog's education and can be taught by whistle, voice and/or hand signals. Mastery of these commands will allow the handler to signal the dog to accomplish certain tasks such as change direction, come in or make a retrieve.

Every hunting dog also must be properly introduced, ideally at an early age, to the sound of gunfire to prevent a gun-shy or gun-nervous dog. It is important to create a positive attitude and response to the sound of gunfire, indeed even to the sight of the shotgun in hand. Improper exposure or introduction to the gun can ruin a good hunting dog and render him useless in the field.

The inexperienced hunter or

Nothing is as alluring to a German Shorthaired Pointer as live birds on a pond. The well-trained GSP will not attack live birds, knowing the difference between a living creature and a downed animal.

novice GSP owner or competitor should avail himself of several good books on training gundogs before attempting to train his dog. One might contact GSP breeders, hunters or field trialers for recommended reading material; perhaps the neophyte could also join local training groups or enlist the help of a trainer.

HEALTH CONCERNS IN GSPs

Prospective owners of any dog should be aware of the potential health problems within their chosen breed. As a breed, the GSP is generally healthy, although some may be prone to epilepsy (seizures), hermaphrodism (having both male and female reproductive

DO YOU WANT TO LIVE LONGER?
If you like to volunteer, it is wonderful if you can take your dog to a nursing home once a week for several hours. The elderly community loves to have a dog with which to visit, and often your dog will bring a bit of companionship to someone who is lonely or somewhat detached from the world. You will be not only bringing happiness to someone else but also keeping your dog busy—and we haven't even mentioned the fact that it has been discovered that volunteering helps to increase your own longevity!

A healthy dog looks healthy; good condition is evident in a fit body, shiny coat, clear eyes and alert, vibrant temperament.

organs) and HD (hip dysplasia), which is the improper formation of the hip joint. Other health concerns are entropion (defect of the eyelid); gastric torsion (sudden dilatation or bloating of the stomach); vWD (von Willebrand's disease), which is a bleeding disorder similar to hemophilia; pannus (corneal inflammation) and OCD (osteochondritis dissecans), which is a cartilage defect of the elbow or shoulder in the growing dog.

Discuss all of these defects with your prospective breeder to be certain that he has screened his sire and dam (and their parents) before breeding. Most of these diseases are of known hereditary cause and, therefore, affected animals should not be included in any breeding program.

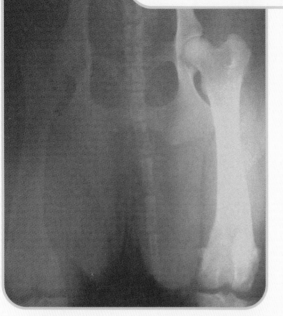

DO YOU KNOW ABOUT HIP DYSPLASIA?

Hip dysplasia is a fairly common condition found in pure-bred dogs. When a dog has hip dysplasia, his hind leg has an incorrectly formed hip joint. By constant use of the hip joint, it becomes more and more loose, wears abnormally and may become arthritic.

Hip dysplasia can only be confirmed with an x-ray, but certain symptoms may indicate a problem. Your dog may have a hip dysplasia problem if he walks in a peculiar manner, hops instead of smoothly runs, uses his hind legs in unison (to keep the pressure off the weak joint), has trouble getting up from a prone position or always sits with both legs together on one side of his body.

As the dog matures, he may adapt well to life with a bad hip, but in a few years the arthritis develops and many dogs with hip dysplasia eventually become crippled.

Hip dysplasia is considered an inherited disease and only can be diagnosed definitively when the dog is two years old. Some experts claim that a special diet might help your puppy outgrow the bad hip, but the usual treatments are surgical. The removal of the pectineus muscle, the removal of the round part of the femur, reconstructing the pelvis and replacing the hip with an artificial one are all surgical interventions that are expensive, but they are usually very successful. Follow the advice of your veterinarian.

Above: X-ray of a dog with "Good" hips.

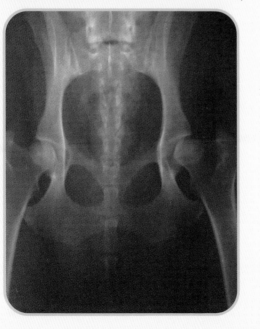

Right: X-ray of a dog with "Moderate" dysplastic hips.

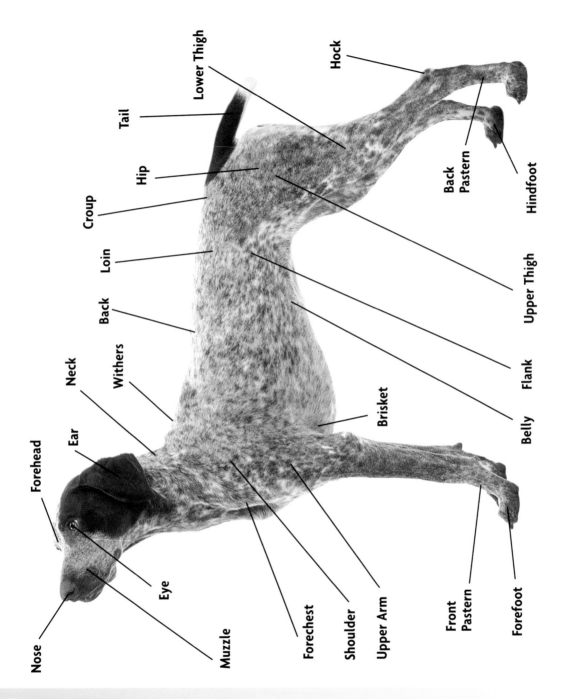

Physical Structure of the German Shorthaired Pointer

GERMAN SHORTHAIRED POINTER

Every recognized breed of dog has a standard, a sort of physical blueprint that has been approved by the American Kennel Club, to illustrate a dog that represents the ideal specimen of each breed. Without such guidelines, breeders could pursue their own personal vision for the breed, a practice that might well suit the breeder, but certainly not the best interests of the breed. The guidelines set forth in the standard are intended not only for the breeders but also for the judges who will assess the dogs at work and in the show ring, and whose opinions can greatly impact the direction of the breed.

There are different standards for each breed, depending on the country. The US abides by the AKC's standard while Germany, the breed's homeland, and the rest of Europe abide by the standard of the Fédération Cynologique Internationale (FCI). There are a few notable differences...and many similarities...between the two standards. While both agree on general

appearance and expression, the AKC standard goes into more detail about the desirable characteristics of a hunting dog. The German standard does not go into such detail, accepting as fact that the breed is and must be a hunter. The German standard also calls for slightly larger dogs and bitches; a more noticeable allowance is given to bitches. The AKC includes a section on gait (movement); this is not mentioned in the FCI standard. The FCI allows black dogs in the same patterns allowed in brown or roan dogs, while the AKC lists black as a disqualification. The AKC also goes into detail about

Dogs competing in dog shows are compared to the breed standard. The dog that most closely conforms to the standard, in the judge's opinion, is the winner.

The GSP is a medium-sized dog with a short back, standing over plenty of ground.

faults and disqualifications, listed along with the descriptions of each point.

Those interested in studying the complete standard of the breed's homeland are advised to obtain a copy of the official FCI standard, which is the standard of Germany. Following the complete AKC standard presented here is an excerpt of the FCI standard for basic comparison purposes.

THE AMERICAN KENNEL CLUB STANDARD FOR THE GERMAN SHORTHAIRED POINTER

The head and skull should be clean-cut, neither too light nor too heavy. The ears must hang close to the head.

General Appearance: The German Shorthaired Pointer is a versatile hunter, an all-purpose gundog capable of high performance in field and water. The judgement of Shorthairs in the show ring reflects this basic characteristic. The overall picture which is created in the observer's eye is that of an aristocratic, well balanced, symmetrical animal with conformation indicating power, endurance and agility and a look of intelligence and animation. The dog is neither unduly small nor conspicuously large. It gives the impression of medium size, but is like the proper hunter, "with a short back, but standing over plenty of ground." Symmetry and field quality are most essential. A dog in hard and lean field condition is not to be penalized; however, overly fat or poorly muscled dogs are to be penalized. A dog well balanced in all points is preferable to one with outstanding good qualities and defects. Grace of outline, clean-cut head, sloping shoulders, deep chest, powerful back, strong quarters, good bone composition, adequate muscle, well carried tail and taut coat produce a look of nobility and indicate a heritage of purposefully conducted breeding. Further evidence of this heritage is movement which is balanced, alertly coordinated and without wasted motion.

Size, Proportion, Substance:
Size—height of dogs, measured at the withers, 23 to 25 inches. Height of bitches, measured at the withers, 21 to 23 inches. Deviations of one inch above or below the described heights are to be severely penalized. Weight of dogs 55 to 70 pounds. Weight of bitches 45 to 60 pounds. *Proportion*—measuring from the forechest to the rearmost projection of the rump and from the withers to the ground, the Shorthair is permissibly either square or slightly longer than he is tall. *Substance*—thin and fine bones are by no means desirable in a dog which must possess strength and be able to work over any type of terrain. The main importance is not laid so much on the size of bone, but rather on the bone being in proper proportion to the body. Bone structure too heavy or too light is a fault. Tall and leggy dogs, dogs which are ponderous because of excess substance, doggy bitches, and bitchy dogs are to be faulted.

Head: The *head* is clean-cut, is neither too light nor too heavy, and is in proper proportion to the body. The *eyes* are of medium size, full of intelligence and expression, good-humored and yet radiating energy, neither protruding nor sunken. The eye is almond shaped, not circular. The preferred color is dark brown.

The GSP's expression contributes to the overall impression of an aristrocratic, balanced, intelligent dog.

Light yellow eyes are not desirable and are a fault. Closely set eyes are to be faulted. China or wall eyes are to be disqualified. The *ears* are broad and set fairly high, lie flat and never hang away from the head. Their placement is just above eye level. The ears, when laid in front without being pulled, should extend to the corner of the mouth. In the case of heavier dogs, the ears are correspondingly longer. Ears too long or fleshy are to be faulted. The *skull* is reasonably broad, arched on the side and slightly round on top. Unlike the Pointer, the median line between the eyes at the forehead is not too deep and the occipital bone is not very conspicuous. The foreface rises gradually from nose to forehead. The rise is more strongly pronounced in the dog than in the bitch. The jaw is powerful and the muscles well developed. The line to the forehead rises gradually and never has a definite stop as that of the Pointer, but rather a stop-effect when viewed from the side, due to the position of the eyebrows. The *muzzle* is sufficiently long to enable the dog to seize game properly and be able to carry it for a long time. A pointed muzzle is not desirable. The depth is in the right proportion to the length, both in the muzzle and in the skull proper. The length of the muzzle should equal the length of skull. A dish-shaped muzzle is a fault. A definite Pointer stop is a serious fault. Too many wrinkles in the forehead is a fault. The *nose* is brown, the larger the better, and with nostrils well opened and broad. A spotted nose is not desirable. A flesh colored nose disqualifies. The chops fall away from the somewhat projecting nose. Lips are full and deep yet are never flewy. The

The solid liver color, without ticking or any white on the body, is less commonly seen than the other color varieties.

teeth are strong and healthy. The molars intermesh properly. The bite is a true scissors bite. A perfect level bite is not desirable and must be penalized. Extreme overshot or undershot disqualifies.

Neck, Topline, Body: The *neck* is of proper length to permit the jaws reaching game to be retrieved, sloping downwards on beautifully curving lines. The nape is rather muscular, becoming gradually larger toward the shoulders. Moderate throatiness is permitted. The *skin* is close and tight. The chest in general gives the impression of depth rather than breadth; for all that, it is in correct proportion to the other parts of the body. The chest reaches down to the elbows, the ribs forming the thorax show a rib spring and are not flat or slab-sided; they are not perfectly round or barrel-shaped. The back ribs reach well down. The circumference of the thorax immediately behind the elbows is smaller than that of the thorax about a hand's breadth behind elbows, so that the upper arm has room for movement. Tuck-up is apparent. The *back* is short, strong, and straight with a slight rise from the root of the tail to the withers. The loin is strong, is of moderate length, and is slightly arched. An excessively long, roached or swayed back must be penalized. The hips are broad with hip sockets wide apart

Incorrect ears; too long and set low.

Correct ears; broad and set fairly high.

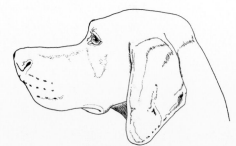

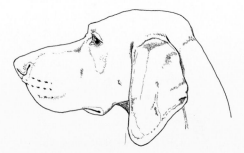

Incorrect muzzle; dish-faced.

Correct muzzle, foreface rising gradually.

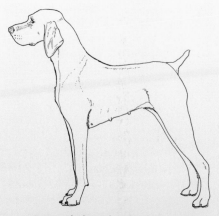

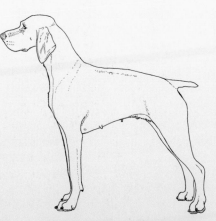

Incorrect body; weak topline, back too short.

Correct body; slight rise from tail to withers.

and fall slightly toward the tail in a graceful curve. A steep croup is a fault. The *tail* is set high and firm, and must be docked, leaving approximately 40% of its length. The tail hangs down when the dog is quiet and is held horizontally when he is walking. The tail must never be curved over the back toward the head when the dog is moving. A tail curved or bent toward the head is to be severely penalized.

Forequarters: The *shoulders* are sloping, movable, and well covered with muscle. The shoulder blades lie flat and are well laid back nearing a 45 degree angle. The upper arm (the bones between the shoulder and elbow joint) is as long as possible, standing away somewhat from the trunk so that the straight and closely muscled legs, when viewed from the front, appear to be parallel. Elbows which stand away from the body or are too close result in toes turning inwards or outwards and must be faulted. *Pasterns* are strong, short and nearly vertical with a slight spring. Loose, short-bladed or straight shoulders must be faulted. Knuckling over is to be faulted. Dewclaws on the forelegs may be removed. The *feet* are compact, close-knit and round to spoon-shaped. The toes are sufficiently arched and heavily nailed. The pads are strong, hard and thick.

> **BREEDING CONSIDERATIONS**
> The decision to breed your dog is one that must be considered carefully and researched thoroughly before moving into action. Some people believe that breeding will make their bitches happier or that it is an easy way to make money. Unfortunately, indiscriminate breeding only worsens the rampant problem of pet overpopulation, as well as putting a considerable dent in your pocketbook. As for the bitch, the entire process from mating through whelping is not an easy one and puts your pet under considerable stress. Last, but not least, consider whether or not you have the means to care for an entire litter of pups. Without a reputation in the field, your attempts to sell the pups may be unsuccessful.

Hindquarters: Thighs are strong and well muscled. Stifles are well bent. Hock joints are well angulated and strong with straight bone structure from hock to pad. Angulation of both stifle and hock joint is such as to achieve the optimal balance of drive and traction. Hocks turn neither in nor out. Cowhocked legs are a serious fault.

Coat: The hair is short and thick and feels tough to the hand; it is somewhat longer on the underside of the tail and the back edges of the haunches. The hair is softer, thinner and shorter on the ears and the head. Any dog with long hair in the body coat is to be severely penalized.

Color: The coat may be of solid liver or a combination of liver and white such as liver and white ticked, liver patched and white ticked, or liver roan. A dog with any area of black, red, orange, lemon or tan, or a dog solid white will be disqualified.

Gait: A smooth lithe gait is essential. It is to be noted that as gait increases from the walk to a faster speed, the legs converge beneath the body. The tendency to single track is desirable. The forelegs reach well ahead as if to pull in the ground without giving the appearance of a hackney gait. The hindquarters drive the back legs smoothly and with great power.

Temperament: The Shorthair is friendly, intelligent, and willing to please. The first impression is that of a keen enthusiasm for work without indication of nervous or flighty character.

Disqualifications:
China or wall eyes.
Flesh colored nose.
Extreme overshot or undershot.
A dog with any area of black, red, orange, lemon, or tan, or a dog solid white.

EXCERPT FROM THE FCI AND GERMAN BREED STANDARD

General Appearance: The general appearance is that of an aristocratic, harmonious dog with a conformation which guarantees endurance, power and agility.

Size: Dogs 62 to 66 cms, measured at the withers. Bitches 58 to 63 cms, measured at the withers.

Head: Dry, clean-cut lines, neither too light nor too heavy, length and size in proportion to the body.

Ears: Moderately long, neither too fleshy nor too fine, broad and high set.

The GSP's gait is smooth and powerful, and the legs converge under the body as the dog picks up speed.

Eyes: Of medium size, neither protruding nor too deep. The preferred color is dark brown.

Nose: Brown; nostrils well opened, broad, movable.

Teeth: Strong, preferably complete dentition and correct positioning of teeth. The incisors should form a scissors bite.

Neck: Of good length in proportion to the body structure, very muscular, slightly arched, gradually broadening towards the shoulders.

Chest and Rib Cage: The chest in general gives the impression of depth instead of breadth, for all that it should be in correct proportion to the other parts of the body.

Back, Loins, Body, Croup: A strong back is particularly important for rapid movement and endurance. Therefore it should not be too long, and the loins should be broad and elastic as well as straight to slightly arched. There should be a slight tuck-up in order to provide adequate room while galloping.

Forequarters: The shoulders should be sloping, dry and well muscled. The shoulder blades should lie flat. The upper arm should be as long as possible.

Hindquarters: The pelvic area should be long, broad and roomy. The upper thigh should be broad and well muscled, the lower thighs and metatarsus correctly angulated.

Feet: Strong and compact, round to oval. Well-arched toes with strong nails, the pads should be strong and hard.

Coat: The skin should be tight without any wrinkles. The coat is short and dense and should be tough and harsh to the touch.

Tail: High set, strong at the base, then tapering; of medium length; however, to avoid injury it should be docked to one-half its length.

Bones: It is not the size of the bones which is essential but rather the composition or density of the bones.

Color: The permissible colors are:
a. Liver without markings.
b. Liver with some white spots or ticking on the chest and legs.
c. Dark roan, with brown head, brown patches or spots.
d. Light roan with a brown head, brown patches or spots.
e. White, with brown markings on the head, large brown patches or spots on the body.
f. Black in the same color patterns as brown or roan.

GERMAN SHORTHAIRED POINTER

PUPPY SELECTION

If you are considering adding a German Shorthaired Pointer puppy to the family, it is important to find the right dog, which of course means finding the right breeder. Start by defining your goals for your pup and whether you hope to spend glorious days together in the field, win blue ribbons in the show ring or just enjoy the companionship of an exuberant and playful canine companion. You should interview breeders who specialize in your preferred type of GSP. Make sure the breeder's experience includes several years involved in the breed activities that interest you, and that he is accomplished in those areas. The breeder should amiably accept your many questions about his experience and should also question you about your intentions with the puppy and whether or not you can provide the pup with a home of which he approves. Good breeders consider their puppies to be a second family and care deeply about the welfare and future of their little ones.

Aside from looking for health, sound temperament and a good genetic background, you should decide if you'd prefer a male or female puppy. For a family companion, a bitch may be the better choice, considering the female's inbred concern for

The best way to predict how your puppy will mature is to observe him with at least one of his parents.

ARE YOU PREPARED?

Unfortunately, when a puppy is bought by someone who does not take into consideration the time and attention that dog ownership requires, it is the puppy who suffers when he is either abandoned or placed in a shelter by a frustrated owner. So all of the "homework" you do in preparation for your pup's arrival will benefit you both. The more informed you are, the more you will know what to expect and the better equipped you will be to handle the ups and downs of raising a puppy. Hopefully, everyone in the household is willing to do his part in raising and caring for the pup. The anticipation of owning a dog often brings a lot of promises from excited family members: "I will walk him every day," "I will feed him," "I will house-train him," etc., but these things take time and effort, and promises can easily be forgotten once the novelty of the new pet has worn off.

all young creatures and her accompanying tolerance and patience. It is always advisable to spay (female) or neuter (male) any dog to be kept solely as a companion, with no intentions for breeding or showing. In fact, responsible breeders will require that all pups sold to pet homes be spayed or neutered at the appropriate age; this will be part of the sales agreement.

When finally selecting your puppy, if the breeder has not already done so for you (and many do), look for the pup who is bold and outgoing, personable and eager to meet you. Beware the pup who tucks his tail and runs or slips away. This is not true GSP temperament, and temperament is primary over all other breed characteristics.

A reliable source for good breeders is your local breed club, qualified vets and the American Kennel Club, which can refer you to breeders and club contacts.

COMMITMENT OF OWNERSHIP

After considering all of the factors concerning owning a dog, and a GSP in particular, you have most likely already made some very important decisions about selecting your puppy. You have chosen the German Shorthaired Pointer as the breed for you, which means that you have decided which characteristics you want in a dog and what type of dog will best fit into your family and lifestyle. If you have selected a breeder, you have gone a step further—you have done your research and found a responsible, conscientious person who breeds quality German Shorthaired Pointers and who should be a reliable source of help as you and your puppy adjust to life together. If you have observed a litter in action, you have obtained a firsthand look at the dynamics of a puppy "pack" and, thus, you should have learned about each pup's individual personality. Perhaps you have even found a pup that particularly appeals to you.

However, even if you have not yet found the German Shorthaired Pointer puppy of your dreams, observing pups will help you learn to recognize certain behavior and to determine what a pup's behavior indicates about his temperament. You will be able to pick out which pups are the leaders, which ones are less outgoing, which ones are confident, which ones are shy, playful, friendly, aggressive, etc. Equally as important, you will learn to recognize what a healthy pup should look and act like. All of these things will help you in your search, and when you find

TEMPERAMENT COUNTS

Your selection of a good puppy can be determined by your needs. A show potential or a good pet? It is your choice. Every puppy, however, should be of good temperament. Although show-quality puppies are bred and raised with emphasis on physical conformation, responsible breeders strive for equally good temperament. Do not buy from a breeder who concentrates solely on physical beauty at the expense of personality.

The German Shorthaired Pointer is a wonderful family dog. Children and GSPs make great companions, providing the children have been instructed how to properly handle the dog.

the German Shorthaired Pointer that was meant for you, you will know it!

Researching your breed, selecting a responsible breeder and observing as many pups as possible are all important steps on the way to dog ownership. It may seem like a lot of effort, and you have not even taken the pup home yet! Remember, though, you cannot be too careful when it comes to deciding on the type of dog you want and finding out about your prospective pup's background. Buying a puppy is not—or *should* not be—just another whimsical

ARE YOU A FIT OWNER?
If the breeder from whom you are buying a puppy asks you a lot of personal questions, do not be insulted. Such a breeder wants to be sure that you will be a fit provider for his puppy.

purchase. This is one instance in which you actually do get to choose your own family! You may be thinking that buying a puppy should be fun—it should not be so serious and so much work. Keep in mind that your puppy is not a cuddly stuffed toy or decorative lawn ornament, but a creature that will become a real member of your family. You will come to realize that, while buying a puppy is a pleasurable and exciting endeavor, it is not something to be taken lightly. Relax...the fun will start when the pup comes home!

Always keep in mind that a puppy is nothing more than a baby in a furry disguise...a baby who is virtually helpless in a human world and who trusts his owner for fulfillment of his basic needs for survival. In addition to water and shelter, your pup needs care, protection, guidance and love. If you are not prepared to commit to this, then you are not prepared to own a dog.

"Wait a minute," you say. "How hard could this be? All of my neighbors own dogs and they seem to be doing just fine. Why should I have to worry about all of this?" Well, you should not worry about it; in fact, you will probably find that once your German Shorthaired Pointer pup gets used to his

PEDIGREE VS. REGISTRATION CERTIFICATE

Too often new owners are confused between these two important documents. Your puppy's pedigree, essentially a family tree, is a written record of a dog's genealogy of three generations or more. The pedigree will show you the names as well as performance titles of all of the dogs in your pup's background. Your breeder must provide you with a registration application, with his part properly filled out. You must complete the application and send it to the AKC with the proper fee. Every puppy must come from a litter that has been AKC-registered by the breeder, born in the US and from a sire and dam that are also registered with the AKC.

The seller must provide you with complete records to identify the puppy. The AKC requires that the seller provide the buyer with the following: breed; sex, color and markings; date of birth; litter number (when available); names and registration numbers of the parents; breeder's name; and date sold or delivered.

PET INSURANCE

Just like you can insure your car, your house and your own health, you likewise can insure your dog's health. Investigate a pet insurance policy by talking to your vet. Depending on the age of your dog, the breed and the kind of coverage you desire, your policy can be very affordable. Most policies cover accidental injuries, poisoning and thousands of medical problems and illnesses, including cancers. Some carriers also offer routine care and immunization coverage.

new home, he will fall into his place in the family quite naturally. But it never hurts to emphasize the commitment of dog ownership. With some time and patience, it is really not too difficult to raise a curious and exuberant German Shorthaired Pointer pup to be a well-adjusted and well-mannered adult dog—a dog that could be your most loyal friend.

PREPARING PUPPY'S PLACE IN YOUR HOME

Researching your breed and finding a breeder are only two aspects of the "homework" you will have to do before taking your German Shorthaired Pointer puppy home. You will also have to prepare your home and family for the new addition.

Much as you would prepare a nursery for a newborn baby, you will need to designate a place in your home that will be the puppy's own. How you prepare your home will depend on how much freedom the dog will be allowed. Whatever you decide, you must ensure that he has a place that he can "call his own."

When you bring your new puppy into your home, you are bringing him into what will become his home as well. Obviously, you did not buy a puppy so that he could "rule the roost" in your home, but in order for a puppy to grow into a stable, well-adjusted dog, he has to feel comfortable in his surroundings. Remember, he is leaving the warmth and security of his mother and littermates, as well as the familiarity of the only place he has ever known, so it is important to make his transition as easy as possible. By preparing a place in your home for the puppy, you are making him feel as welcome as possible in a strange new place. It should not take him long to get used to it, but the sudden shock of being transplanted is somewhat traumatic for a young pup. Imagine how a small child would feel in the same situation—that is how your puppy must be feeling. It is up to you to reassure him and to let him know, "Little *hund*, you are going to like it here!"

WHAT YOU SHOULD BUY

CRATE

To someone unfamiliar with the use of crates in dog training, it may seem like punishment to shut a dog in a crate, but this is not the case at all. Most breeders and trainers recommend crates as preferred tools for pet puppies as well as show puppies. Crates are not cruel—crates have many humane and highly effective uses in dog care and training. For example, crate training is a very popular and very successful housebreaking method. A crate can keep your dog safe during travel and, perhaps most importantly, a crate provides your dog with a place of his own in your home. It serves as a "doggie bedroom" of sorts—your German Short-haired Pointer can curl up in his crate when he wants to sleep or when he just needs a break. Many dogs sleep in their crates overnight. With soft bedding and his favorite toy, a crate becomes a cozy pseudo-den for your dog. Like his ancestors, he too will seek out the comfort and retreat of a den—you just happen to be providing him with something a little more luxurious than what his early ancestors enjoyed.

As far as purchasing a crate, the type that you buy is up to you. It will most likely be one of

YOUR SCHEDULE . . .
If you lead an erratic, unpredictable life, with daily or weekly changes in your work requirements, consider the problems of owning a dog. The new puppy has to be fed regularly, socialized (loved, petted, handled, introduced to other people) and, most importantly, allowed to go outdoors often for house-training. As the dog gets older, he can become more tolerant of deviations in his feeding times and relief schedule.

Your local pet shop should have a selection of crates from which you can make a suitable choice for your GSP.

PHOTO COURTESY OF DOSKOCIL

seems as if they grow right before your eyes. A small crate may be fine for a very young German Shorthaired Pointer pup, but it will not do him

The crate you purchase when your GSP is a puppy should be large enough for the full-grown dog.

the two most popular types: wire or fiberglass. There are advantages and disadvantages to each type. For example, a wire crate is more open, allowing the air to flow through and affording the dog a view of what is going on around him, while a fiberglass crate is sturdier. Both can double as travel crates, providing protection for the dog.

The size of the crate is another thing to consider. Puppies do not stay puppies forever—in fact, sometimes it

much good for long! Unless you have the money and the inclination to buy a new crate every time your pup has a growth spurt, it is better to get one that will accommodate your dog both as a pup and at full size. A medium- to large-size crate will be necessary for a full-grown German Shorthaired Pointer, who stands up to 25 inches high.

BEDDING

Soft bedding or a crate pad in the dog's crate will help the dog feel more at home, and you may also like to give him a small blanket. These things will take the place of the leaves, twigs, etc., that the pup would use in the wild to make a den; the pup can make his own "burrow" in the crate. Although your pup is far removed from his den-making ancestors, the denning instinct is still a part of his genetic makeup. Second, until you take your pup home, he has been sleeping amid the warmth of his mother and littermates, and while a blanket is not the same as a warm, breathing body, it still provides heat and something with which to snuggle. You will want to wash your pup's bedding frequently in case he has an "accident" in his crate, and replace anything in his crate that becomes ragged and starts to fall apart.

CRATE-TRAINING TIPS

During crate training, you should partition off the section of the crate in which the pup stays. If he is given too big an area, this will hinder your training efforts. Crate training is based on the fact that a dog does not like to soil his sleeping quarters, so it is ineffective to keep a pup in a crate that is so big that he can eliminate at one end and get far enough away from his droppings to sleep. Also, you want to make the crate den-like for the pup. Blankets and a favorite toy will make the crate cozy for the small pup; as he grows, you may want to evict some of his "roommates" to make more room. It will take some coaxing at first, but be patient. Given some time to get used to it, your pup will adapt to his new home-within-a-home quite nicely.

TOYS, TOYS, TOYS!

With a big variety of dog toys available, and so many that look like they would be a lot of fun for a dog, be careful in your selection. It is amazing what a set of puppy teeth can do to an innocent-looking toy; so, obviously, safety is a major consideration. Be sure to choose the most durable products that you can find. Hard nylon bones and toys are a safe bet, and many of them are offered in different scents and flavors that will be sure to capture your dog's attention. It is always fun to play a game of fetch with your dog, and there are balls and flying discs that are specially made to withstand dog teeth.

Toys

Toys are a must for dogs of all ages, especially for curious playful pups. Puppies are the "children" of the dog world, and what child does not love toys? Chew toys provide enjoyment for both dog and owner—your dog will enjoy playing with his favorite toys, while you will enjoy the fact that they distract him from your expensive shoes and leather couch. Puppies love to chew; in fact, chewing is a physical need for pups as they are teething, and everything looks appetizing! The full range of your possessions—from old dish rag to Oriental carpet—are fair game in the eyes of a teething pup. Puppies are not all that discerning when it comes to finding something to literally "sink their teeth into"— everything tastes great!

German Shorthaired Pointer puppies are fairly aggressive chewers and only the sturdiest, strongest toys should be offered to them. Breeders advise owners to resist stuffed toys, except under supervision, because they can become de-stuffed in no time. The overly excited pup may ingest the stuffing, which is neither nutritious nor digestible.

Similarly, squeaky toys are popular, but must be avoided for the German Shorthaired Pointer. Perhaps a squeaky toy can be used as an aid in training, but not for free play. If a pup "disembowels" one of these, the small plastic squeaker inside can be dangerous if swallowed. Monitor the condition of all your pup's toys carefully and get rid of any that have been chewed to the point of becoming potentially dangerous.

Be careful of natural bones, which have a tendency to splinter into sharp, dangerous pieces. Also be careful of rawhide, which can turn into pieces that are easy to swallow and can also become a mushy mess on your carpet.

LEASH

A nylon leash is probably the best option, as it is the most resistant to puppy teeth should your pup take a liking to chewing on his leash. Of course, this is a habit that should be nipped in the bud, but, if your pup likes to chew on his leash, he has a very slim chance of being able to chew through the strong nylon. Nylon leashes are also lightweight, which is good for a young German Shorthaired Pointer who is just getting used to the idea of walking on a leash. For everyday walking and safety purposes, the nylon leash is a good choice.

As your pup grows up and gets used to walking on the leash, you may want to purchase a flexible leash. These

MENTAL AND DENTAL

Toys not only help your puppy get the physical and mental stimulation he needs but also provide a great way to keep his teeth clean. Hard rubber or nylon toys, especially those constructed with grooves, are designed to scrape away plaque, preventing bad breath and gum infection.

Soft toys are often enjoyed by pups and adults alike, but, as soft toys can be destroyed easily, supervision is necessary when your GSP is playing with them.

leashes allow you to extend the length to give the dog a broader area to explore or to shorten the length to keep the dog near you. Of course there are special leashes for training purposes, but these are not necessary for routine walks.

COLLAR

Your pup should get used to wearing a collar all the time since you will want to attach his ID tags to it. Plus, you have to attach the leash to something! A lightweight nylon collar is a good choice; make sure that it fits snugly enough so that the pup cannot wriggle out of it, but is loose enough so that it will

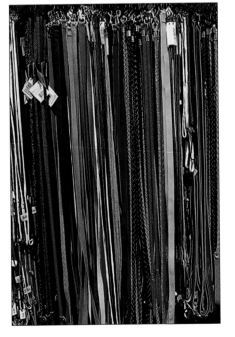

From the wide selections of leashes available, select a sturdy yet lightweight leash for everyday use with your GSP.

> **FINANCIAL RESPONSIBILITY**
> Grooming tools, collars, leashes, crates, dog beds and, of course, toys will be expenses to you when you first obtain your pup, and the cost will continue throughout your dog's lifetime. If your puppy damages or destroys your possessions (as most puppies surely will!) or something belonging to a neighbor, you can calculate additional expense. There is also flea and pest control, which every dog owner faces more than once. You must be able to handle the financial responsibility of owning a dog.

not be uncomfortably tight around the pup's neck. You should be able to fit a finger between the pup and the collar. It may take some time for your pup to get used to wearing the collar, but soon he will not even notice that it is there. Choke collars are made for training, but should only be used by those who have been instructed in their proper use and *only* during training.

FOOD AND WATER BOWLS

Your pup will need two bowls, one for food and one for water. You may want two sets of bowls, one for inside and one for outside, depending on where the dog will be fed and where he will be spending time. Stainless steel or sturdy plastic bowls

CHOOSE AN APPROPRIATE COLLAR

The BUCKLE COLLAR is the standard collar used for everyday purposes. Be sure that you adjust the buckle on growing puppies. Check it every day. It can become too tight overnight! These collars can be made of leather or nylon. Attach your dog's identification tags to this collar.

The CHOKE COLLAR is the designed for training. It is constructed of highly polished steel so that it slides easily through the stainless steel loop. The idea is that the dog controls the pressure around his neck and will stop pulling if the collar becomes uncomfortable. *Never* leave a choke collar on your dog when not training.

The HALTER is for a trained dog that has to be restrained to prevent running away, chasing a cat and the like. Considered the most humane of all collars, it is frequently used on smaller dogs on which collars are not comfortable.

are popular choices. Plastic bowls are more chewable, but dogs tend not to chew on the steel variety, which can be sterilized. It is important to buy sturdy bowls since anything is in danger of being chewed by puppy teeth and you do not want your dog to be constantly chewing apart his bowl (for his safety and for your wallet!).

Bowl stands, which elevate the bowls to reduce the amount of air swallowed, should be considered mandatory to protect the deep-chested GSP from the potentially fatal bloat (gastric torsion).

CLEANING SUPPLIES
Until a pup is housebroken, you will be doing a lot of cleaning. "Accidents" will occur, which is acceptable in the beginning because the puppy does not know any better. All you can do is be prepared to clean up any accidents. Old rags, paper towels, newspapers and a safe disinfectant are good to have on hand.

BEYOND THE BASICS
The items previously discussed are the bare necessities. You will find out what else you need as you go along—grooming supplies, flea/tick protection, baby gates to partition a room, etc. These things will vary depending on your situation,

FEEDING TIPS

You will probably start feeding your pup the same food that he has been getting from the breeder; the breeder should give you a few days' supply to start you off. Your breeder also can advise you about a good diet for your adult GSP, based on the diets with which he has had success in his own dogs. Treats are helpful motivators and rewards, but don't overdo it! Try to find healthy dog treats, but remember that too many treats, when given in addition to your dog's regular meals, can lead to weight gain.

It is your responsibility to clean up after your dog has relieved himself. Pet shops have various aids to assist in the cleanup job.

but it is important that you have everything you need to feed and make your German Shorthaired Pointer comfortable in his first few days at home.

PUPPY-PROOFING YOUR HOME

Aside from making sure that your German Shorthaired Pointer will be comfortable in your home, you also have to make sure that your home is safe for your German Short-haired Pointer. This means taking precautions that your pup will not get into anything he should not get into and that there is nothing within his reach that may harm him should he sniff it, chew it, inspect it,

SKULL & CROSSBONES
Never use cockroach or rodent poisons or plant fertilizers in any area accessible to your dog. Avoid the use of toilet cleaners. Most dogs are born with "toilet-bowl sonar" and will take a drink if the lid is left open. Also make sure that the garbage cans are securely closed and out of reach.

Scour your garage for potential doggy dangers. Remove weed killers, pesticides and antifreeze materials from any area to which the dog has access. Antifreeze is highly toxic and just a few drops can kill a puppy or an adult dog. The sweet taste attracts the animal, who will quickly consume it from the floor or pavement.

etc. This probably seems obvious since, while you are primarily concerned with your pup's safety, at the same time you do not want your belongings to be ruined. Breakables should be placed out of reach if your dog

is to have full run of the house. If he is to be limited to certain places within the house, keep any potentially dangerous items in the "off-limits" areas. An electrical cord can pose a danger should the puppy decide to taste it—and who is going to convince a pup that it would not make a great chew toy? Cords should be fastened tightly against the wall to be kept from puppy teeth. If your dog is going to spend time in a crate, make sure that there is nothing near his crate that he can reach if he sticks his curious little nose or paws through the openings. Just as you would with a child, keep all household cleaners and chemicals where the pup cannot reach them.

It is also important to make sure that the outside of your home is safe. Of course, your puppy should never be unsupervised, but a pup let loose in the yard will want to run and explore, and he should be granted that freedom. Do not let a fence give you a false sense of security; you would be surprised how crafty (and persistent) a dog can be in working out how to dig under and squeeze his way through small holes, or to jump or climb over a fence. The remedy is to make the fence well embedded into the ground and high enough so that it really is impossible for your dog to get over it (at least 6 feet is necessary). It is not uncommon for a German Shorthaired Pointer to scale a fence less than 6 feet tall. Be sure to repair or secure any gaps in the fence. Check the fence periodically to ensure that it is in good shape and make repairs as needed; a very determined pup may return to the same spot to "work on it" until he is able to get through.

FIRST TRIP TO THE VET

You have selected your puppy, and your home and family are ready. Now all you have to do is collect your German Shorthaired Pointer from the breeder and the fun begins, right? Well...not so fast. Something else you need to prepare is your pup's first trip to the veterinarian. Perhaps the breeder can recommend someone in the area who specializes in German Shorthaired Pointers or pointer breeds, or maybe you know some other German Shorthaired Pointer owners who can suggest a good vet. Either way, you should have an appointment arranged for your pup before you pick him up.

The pup's first visit will consist of an overall examination to make sure that the pup does not have any problems that are not apparent to you. The veterinarian will also set up a schedule for the pup's vaccina-

tions; the breeder will inform you of which ones the pup has already received and the vet can continue from there.

INTRODUCTION TO THE FAMILY

Everyone in the house will be excited about the puppy's coming home and will want to

HOW VACCINES WORK

If you've just bought a puppy, you surely know the importance of having your pup vaccinated, but do you understand how vaccines work? Vaccines contain the same bacteria or viruses that cause the disease you want to prevent, but they have been chemically modified so that they don't cause any harm. Instead, the vaccine causes your dog to produce antibodies that fight the harmful bacteria. Thus, if your dog is exposed to the disease in the future, the antibodies will destroy the viruses or bacteria.

pet him and play with him, but it is best to keep the introduction low-key so as not to overwhelm the puppy. He is apprehensive already. It is the first time he has been separated from his mother and the breeder, and the ride to your home is likely to be the first time he has been in a car. The last thing you want to do is smother him, as this will only frighten him further. This is not to say that human contact is not extremely necessary at this stage, because this is the time when a connection between the pup and his human family is formed. Gentle petting

TOXIC PLANTS

Many plants can be toxic to dogs. If you see your dog carrying a piece of vegetation in his mouth, approach him in a quiet, disinterested manner, avoid eye contact, pet him and gradually remove the plant from his mouth. Alternatively, offer him a treat and maybe he'll drop the plant on his own accord. Be sure no toxic plants are growing in your own yard or garden.

Loyalty to the whole family defines the GSP, and there is no better bond than that between children and a dog that has grown up with them.

and soothing words should help console him, as well as just putting him down and letting him explore on his own (under your watchful eye, of course).

The pup may approach the family members or may busy himself with exploring for a while. Gradually, each person should spend some time with the pup, one at a time, crouching down to get as close to the pup's level as possible, letting the pup sniff his hands and petting him gently. He definitely needs human attention and he needs to be touched—this is how to form an immediate bond. Just remember that the pup is experiencing a lot of things for the first time, at the same time. There are new people, new noises, new smells and new things to investigate, so be gentle, be affectionate and be as comforting as you can be.

PUP'S FIRST NIGHT HOME

You have traveled home with your new charge safely in his crate. He's been to the vet for a thorough check-up; he's been weighed, his papers examined; perhaps he's even been vaccinated and wormed as well. He's met the family and he's licked the whole family, including the excited children and the less-than-happy cat. He's explored his area, his new bed, the yard and anywhere else he's been

permitted. He's eaten his first meal at home and relieved himself in the proper place. He's heard lots of new sounds, smelled new friends and seen more of the outside world than ever before.

That was just the first day! He's worn out and is ready for bed...or so you think!

It's puppy's first night and you are ready to say "Good night"—keep in mind that this is the pup's first night ever to be sleeping alone. His dam and littermates are no longer at paw's length and he's a bit scared, cold and lonely. Be reassuring to your new family member, but this is not the time to spoil him and give in to his inevitable whining.

Puppies whine. They whine to let others know where they

GSPs are excellent jumpers; keep this in mind when erecting a fence to ensure it is of sufficient height to contain the dog.

TIME TO GO HOME
Breeders rarely release puppies until they are eight to ten weeks of age. This is an acceptable age for most breeds of dog, excepting toy breeds, which are not released until around 12 weeks, given their petite sizes. If a breeder has a puppy that is 12 weeks of age or older, he is likely well socialized and house-trained. Be sure that he is otherwise healthy before deciding to take him home.

are and hopefully to get company out of it. Place your pup in his new bed or crate in his room and close the crate door. Mercifully, he may fall asleep without a peep. When the inevitable occurs, ignore the whining; he is fine. Be strong and keep his interest in mind. Do not allow yourself to feel guilty and visit the pup. He will quiet down and fall asleep eventually.

Many breeders recommend placing a piece of bedding from the pup's former home in his new bed so that he recognizes the scent of his littermates. Others still advise placing a hot water bottle in his bed for warmth. This latter may be a good idea provided the pup doesn't attempt to suckle—he'll get good and wet and may not fall asleep so fast.

Puppy's first night can be somewhat stressful for the pup and his new family. Remember that you are setting the tone of nighttime at your house. Unless you want to play with your pup every night at 10 p.m., midnight and 2 a.m., don't initiate the habit. Your family will thank you, and eventually so will your pup!

PREVENTING PUPPY PROBLEMS

SOCIALIZATION
Now that you have done all of the preparatory work and have helped your pup get accustomed to his new home and family, it is about time for you to have some fun! Socializing your German Shorthaired Pointer pup gives you the opportunity to show off your new friend, and your pup gets to reap the benefits of being an adorable, charming creature that people will

Those insatiable teeth are something that every puppy owner faces! You'd be surprised at what your pup finds "chew-worthy."

want to pet and, in general, think is absolutely precious!

Besides getting to know his new family, your puppy should be exposed to other people, animals and situations, but of course he must not come into close contact with dogs you don't know well until his course of injections is fully complete. Socialization will help your puppy become well adjusted as he grows up and less prone to being timid or fearful of the new things he will encounter. Your pup's socialization began with the breeder, but now it is your responsibility to continue it. The socialization he receives up until the age of 12 weeks is the most critical, as this is the time when he forms his impressions of the outside world. Be especially careful during the eight-to-ten-week-old period, also known as the fear period. The

BEATING BOREDOM

Your fenced-in yard is a wonderful place for your German Shorthaired Pointer to exercise himself and run off some energy, but this is not a breed to be left for hours on end alone in the yard. He thrives on time spent with his owners, and, if left alone for too long, can become bored and develop destructive behaviors, and may even devote his considerable skills to escaping from the yard.

interaction he receives during this time should be especially gentle and reassuring. Lack of socialization can manifest itself in fear and aggression as the dog grows up. He needs lots of human contact, affection,

PROPER SOCIALIZATION

The socialization period for puppies is from age 8 to 16 weeks. This is the time when puppies need to leave their birth family and take up residence with their new owners, where they will meet many new people, other pets, etc. Failure to be adequately socialized can cause the dog to grow up fearing others and being shy and unfriendly due to a lack of self-confidence. A well-socialized dog should remain well-behaved in unfamiliar situations and should be eager and inquisitive about new experiences.

handling and exposure to other animals.

Once your pup has received his necessary vaccinations, feel free to take him out and about (on his leash, of course). Walk him around the neighborhood, take him on your daily errands, let people pet him, let him meet other dogs and pets, etc. Puppies do not have to try to make friends; there will be no shortage of people who will want to introduce themselves. Just make sure that you carefully supervise each meeting. If the neighborhood children want to say hello, for example, that is great—children and German Shorthairs are known to make great companions. However, sometimes an excited child can unintentionally handle a pup too roughly, or an overzealous pup can playfully nip a little too hard. You want to make socialization experiences positive ones. What a pup learns during this very formative stage will affect his attitude toward future encounters. You want your dog to be comfortable around everyone. A pup that has a bad experience with a child may grow up to be a dog that is shy around or aggressive toward children.

CONSISTENCY IN TRAINING
Dogs, being pack animals, naturally need a leader, or else they try to establish dominance in

GSPs are gregarious and enjoy the company of other dogs. This GSP is enjoying an afternoon chat with a Bulldog.

DOG MEETS WORLD
Thorough socialization includes not only meeting new people but also being introduced to new experiences such as riding in the car, having his coat brushed, hearing the television, walking in a crowd—the list is endless. The more your pup experiences, and the more positive the experiences are, the less of a shock and the less frightening it will be for your GSP to encounter new things as an adult.

dominance, coupled with the fact that it is nearly impossible to look at an adorable German Shorthaired Pointer pup with his "puppy-dog" eyes and not cave in, give the pup an almost unfair advantage in getting the upper hand!

A pup will definitely test the waters to see what he can and cannot do. Do not give in to those pleading eyes—stand your ground when it comes to disciplining the pup and make sure that all family members do the same. It will only confuse the pup when Mother tells him to get off the couch when he is used to sitting up there with Father to watch the nightly news. Avoid discrepancies by having all members of the household decide on the rules before the pup even comes home...and be consistent in enforcing them! Early training shapes the dog's personality, so you cannot be unclear in what you expect.

COMMON PUPPY PROBLEMS
The best way to prevent puppy problems is to be proactive in stopping an undesirable behavior as soon as it starts. The old saying "You can't teach an old dog new tricks" does not necessarily hold true, but it *is* true that it is much easier to discourage bad behavior in a young developing pup than to wait

their packs. When you welcome a dog into your family, the choice of who becomes the leader and who becomes the "pack" is entirely up to you! Your pup's intuitive quest for

until the pup's bad behavior becomes the adult dog's bad habit. There are some problems that are especially prevalent in puppies as they develop.

NIPPING

As puppies start to teethe, they feel the need to sink their teeth into anything that's available... unfortunately, that includes your fingers, arms, hair and toes. You may find this behavior cute for the first five seconds... until you feel just how sharp those puppy teeth are. This is something you want to discourage immediately and consistently with a firm "No!" (or whatever number of firm "Nos" it takes for him to understand

THE COCOA WARS

Treats are helpful motivators and rewards in training, but *never* offer chocolate. Chocolate contains the chemical thebromine, which is poisonous to dogs, although "chocolates" especially made for dogs are safe (as they don't actually contain chocolate) but not recommended. Any item that encourages your dog to enjoy the taste of cocoa should be discouraged. You should also exercise caution when using mulch in your garden. This frequently contains cocoa hulls, and dogs have been known to die from eating mulch.

A soft bed and a toy will be much appreciated by your GSP pup as he settles into his new home.

that you mean business). Then replace your finger with an appropriate chew toy. While this behavior is merely annoying when the dog is young, it can become dangerous as your German Shorthaired Pointer's adult teeth grow in and his jaws develop, and he continues to think it is okay to gnaw on

A friendly sniff hello! A properly socialized GSP should get along well with other animals, including other pets in the home, friends' pets and unfamiliar dogs you may meet while out for a walk.

when you are out of the house and he is in his crate or when you are in another part of the house and he cannot see you. The noise he is making is an expression of the anxiety he feels at being alone, so he needs to be taught that being alone is okay. You are not actually training the dog to stop making noise, you are training him to feel comfortable when he is alone and thus removing the need for him to make the noise.

This is where the crate with cozy bedding and a toy comes in handy. You want to know that human appendages. Your German Shorthaired Pointer does not mean any harm with a friendly nip, but he also does not know that a friendly nip can hurt!

CRYING/WHINING

Your pup will often cry, whine, whimper, howl or make some type of commotion when he is left alone. This is basically his way of calling out for attention to make sure that you know he is there and that you have not forgotten about him. He feels insecure when he is left alone,

MANNERS MATTER
During the socialization process, a puppy should meet people, experience different environments and definitely be exposed to other canines. Through playing and interacting with other dogs, your puppy will learn lessons, ranging from controlling the pressure of his jaws by biting his littermates to the inner-workings of the canine pack that he will apply to his relationships with humans and other dogs for the rest of his life. That is why removing a puppy from his litter too early (before eight weeks) can be detrimental to the pup's development.

CHEWING TIPS

Chewing goes hand in hand with nipping in the sense that a teething puppy is always looking for a way to soothe his aching gums. In this case, instead of chewing on you, he may have taken a liking to your favorite shoe or something else which he should not be chewing. Again, realize that this is a normal canine behavior that does not need to be discouraged, only redirected. Your pup just needs to be taught what is acceptable to chew on and what is off-limits. Consistently tell him "No!" when you catch him chewing on something forbidden and give him a chew toy.

Conversely, praise him when you catch him chewing on something appropriate. In this way, you are discouraging the inappropriate behavior and reinforcing the desired behavior. The puppy's chewing should stop after his adult teeth have come in, but an adult dog continues to chew for various reasons—perhaps because he is bored, needs to relieve tension or just likes to chew. That is why it is important to redirect his chewing when he is still young.

important that the crate is never used as a form of punishment, or the pup will have a negative association with the crate.

Accustom the pup to the crate in short, gradually increasing time intervals in which you put him in the crate, maybe with a treat, and stay in the room with him. If he cries or makes a fuss, do not go to him, but stay in his sight. Gradually he will realize that staying in his crate is okay without your help, and it will not be so traumatic for him when you are not around. You may want to leave the radio on softly when you leave the house; the sound of human voices may be comforting to him.

Welcoming a GSP into your home and family means the beginning of a wonderful friendship.

he is safe when you are not there to supervise, and you know that he will be safe in his crate rather than roaming freely around the house. In order for the pup to stay in his crate without making a fuss, he needs to be comfortable in his crate. On that note, it is extremely

DIETARY AND FEEDING CONSIDERATIONS

Today the choices of food for your German Shorthaired Pointer are many and varied. There are simply dozens of brands of food in all sorts of flavors and textures, ranging from puppy diets to those for seniors. There are even hypoallergenic and low-calorie diets available. Because your German Shorthaired Pointer's food has a bearing on coat, health and

temperament, it is essential that the most suitable diet is selected for a German Shorthaired Pointer of his age. It is fair to say, however, that even experienced owners can be perplexed by the enormous range of foods available. Only understanding what is best for your dog will help you reach an informed decision.

Dog foods are produced in three basic types: dry, semi-moist and canned. Dry foods are useful for the cost-conscious for overall they tend to be less expensive than semi-moist or canned. They also contain the least fat and the most preservatives. In general, canned foods are made up of 60–70% water, while semi-moist ones often contain so much sugar that they are perhaps the least preferred by owners, even though their dogs seem to like them.

When selecting your dog's diet, three stages of development must be considered: the puppy stage, the adult stage and the senior stage.

CHANGE IN DIET

As your dog's caretaker, you know the importance of keeping his diet consistent, but sometimes when you run out of food or if you're on vacation, you have to make a change quickly. Some dogs will experience digestive problems, but most will not. If you are planning on changing your dog's menu, do so gradually to ensure that your dog will not have any problems. Over a period of four to five days, slowly add some new food to your dog's old food, increasing the percentage of new food each day.

PUPPY STAGE

Puppies instinctively want to suck milk from their mother's teats and a normal puppy will exhibit this behavior from just a few moments following birth. If puppies do not attempt to suckle within the first half-hour or so, the breeder should encourage them to do so by placing them on the nipples, having selected ones with plenty of milk. This early milk supply is important in providing colostrum to protect the puppies during the first eight to ten weeks of their lives.

Although a mother's milk is much better than any milk formula, despite there being some excellent ones available, if the puppies do not feed, the breeder will have to feed them himself. For those with less experience, advice from a veterinarian is important so that not only the right quantity of milk is fed but also that of correct quality, fed at suitably frequent intervals, usually every two hours during the first few days of life.

Puppies should be allowed to nurse from their mothers for about the first six weeks, although from the third or fourth week the breeder will begin to introduce small portions of suitable solid food. Most breeders like to introduce alternate milk and meat meals

STORING DOG FOOD
You must store your dry dog food carefully. Open packages of dog food quickly lose their vitamin value, usually within 90 days of being opened. Mold spores and vermin could also contaminate the food.

initially, building up to weaning time.

By the time the puppies are seven or a maximum of eight weeks old, they should be fully weaned and fed solely on a proprietary puppy food. Selection of the most suitable, good-quality diet at this time is essential, for a puppy's fastest growth rate is during the first year of life. Your veterinarian and your breeder are able to offer advice about a good puppy food for the GSP. The frequency of meals will be reduced over time, and when a young dog has reached the age of about 12 months he can be switched to an adult diet.

Puppy and junior diets should be well balanced for the needs of your dog, so that, except in certain circumstances, additional vitamins, minerals and proteins will not be required. A growing pup should be kept lean to avoid the possibility of developing joint diseases, problems that can be

TEST FOR PROPER DIET

A good test for proper diet is the color, odor and firmness of your dog's stool. A healthy dog usually produces three semi-hard stools per day. The stools should have no unpleasant odor. They should be the same color from excretion to excretion.

influenced by excess weight, which will stress joints that are not yet fully formed.

ADULT DIETS

Once the pup has reached adult size, at about one year of age, you can switch to a quality adult or performance food, depending on the dog's activity level at the time. Performance foods are best for the active dog who engages in strenuous or high-energy activities. It is seldom wise to add supplements such as vitamins or other additives to your puppy or adult dog's food unless advised to do so by your veterinarian. A quality dog food is properly balanced for healthy growth and maintenance, and any supplements will upset that balance and could in fact be harmful to the dog. Always feed your German Shorthaired Pointer a quality dog food designed for his individual growth and energy requirements. Many dog food manufacturers have designed foods specifically for each canine size group: small-, medium- and large-breed diets that provide the proper fat and protein balance for healthy growth, maintenance and complete nutrition.

SENIOR DIETS

As dogs get older, their metabolism changes. The older dog

Select your puppy's food carefully, as diet plays a vital role in proper development during his growth period.

usually exercises less, moves more slowly and sleeps more. This change in lifestyle and physiological performance requires a change in diet. Since these changes take place slowly, they might not be recognizable. What is easily recognizable is weight gain. By continuing to feed your dog an adult-maintenance diet when he is slowing down metabolically, your dog will gain weight. Obesity in an older dog compounds the health problems that already accompany old age.

As your dog gets older, few of his organs function up to par. The kidneys slow down and the intestines become less efficient. These age-related factors are best handled with a change in diet and a change in feeding

"DOES THIS COLLAR MAKE ME LOOK FAT?"

While humans may obsess about how they look and how trim their bodies are, many people believe that extra weight on their dogs is a good thing. The truth is, pets should not be over- or underweight, as both can lead to or signal sickness. In order to tell how fit your pet is, run your hands over his ribs. Are his ribs buried under a layer of fat or are they sticking out considerably? If your pet is within his normal weight range, you should be able to feel the ribs easily, but they should not protrude abnormally. If you stand above him, the outline of his body should resemble an hourglass. Some breeds do tend to be leaner while some are a bit stockier, but making sure your dog is the right weight for his breed will certainly contribute to his good health.

cially if you feed dry food. Make certain that the dog's water bowl is clean, and change the water often.

EXERCISE
Exercise is an extremely vital component in successfully raising and training your German Shorthaired Pointer. An unexercised GSP will become bored and destructive, and all his

For deep-chested breeds like the GSP, a bowl stand is advisable to avoid the dog's having to crane his neck to eat, thus minimizing the possibilities of bloat (gastric torsion).

schedule to give smaller portions that are more easily digested. Your vet can advise you on when it's time to make dietary changes related to aging.

There is no single best diet for every older dog. While many dogs do well on light or senior diets, other dogs do better on other special premium diets. Be sensitive to your senior GSP's diet and this will help control other problems that may arise with your old friend.

WATER
Just as your dog needs proper nutrition from his food, water is an essential "nutrient" as well. Water keeps the dog's body properly hydrated and promotes normal function of the body's systems. During housebreaking, it is necessary to keep an eye on how much water your German Shorthaired Pointer is drinking, but once he is reliably trained he should have access to clean fresh water at all times, espe-

GRAIN-BASED DIETS
Some less expensive dog foods are based on grains and other plant proteins. While these products may appear to be attractively priced, many breeders prefer a diet based on animal proteins and believe that they are more conducive to your dog's health. Many grain-based diets rely on soy protein, which may cause flatulence (passing gas).

There are many cases, however, when your dog might require a special diet. These special requirements should only be recommended by your veterinarian.

A Worthy Investment

Veterinary studies have proven that a balanced high-quality diet pays off in your dog's coat quality, behavior and activity level. Invest in premium brands that offer complete nutrition for the maximum payoff with your dog.

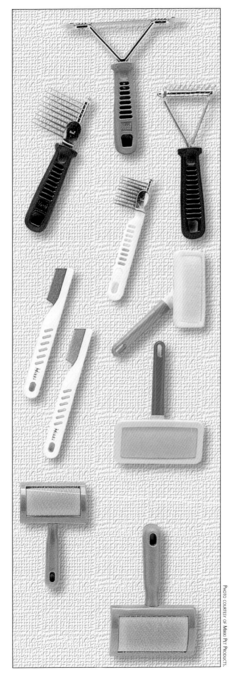

Your local pet shop will have a variety of grooming tools from which you can select what you need for maintaining your GSP's coat in prime condition.

PHOTO COURTESY OF MIKKI PET PRODUCTS.

pent-up energy will make training exceedingly difficult. For the adult GSP, long runs twice daily will satisfy his energy needs; leisurely walks around a few blocks are not sufficient. GSPs are best suited to families who pursue jogging or running as a pastime and enjoy frequent outdoor activities and games such as hiking, swimming, rigorous games of Frisbee or other workout activities.

For the GSP puppy, strenuous exercise or too much exercise is not advised, as this will put stress on his growing frame and can cause bone and/or joint problems. Puppies usually get sufficient exercise by playing in the yard, exploring and just being puppies! As the pup grows up, you can increase his exercise, and by the time he's reached adulthood he will be ready to take on all types of activities.

GROOMING
The German Shorthaired Pointer is considered an "easy keeper" who is easy to groom and requires very little coat attention. Regular brushing with a firm bristle brush will keep the coat healthy, and a good rub with a chamois will give it a lovely shine. Routine bathing should be done only when necessary. The short coat does shed, but shedding can be

controlled with minimal brushing. Feet should be checked regularly for nettles or burrs after a day afield. Always dry the coat thoroughly after bathing, hunting or an outdoor outing to prevent chilling.

Bathing your GSP frequently is neither necessary nor recommended, but there certainly will be times when a bath is called for.

BATHING

Dogs do not need to be bathed as often as humans, but bathing when necessary is important for healthy skin and a clean, shiny coat. Again, like most anything, if you accustom your pup to being bathed as a puppy, it will be second nature by the time he grows up. You want your dog to be at ease in the bath or else the occasional bath times could end up wet, soapy, messy ordeals for both of you!

GROOMING EQUIPMENT

How much grooming equipment you purchase will depend on how much grooming you are going to do. Here are some basics:

- Natural bristle brush
- Chamois
- Rubber mat
- Dog shampoo
- Spray hose attachment
- Towels
- Ear cleaner
- Cotton balls
- Nail clippers
- Canine toothbrush
- Canine toothpaste

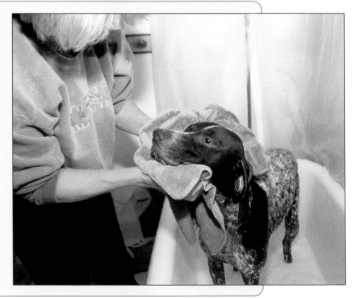

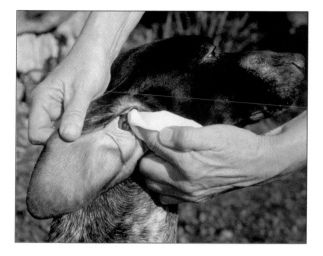

Above: The ears should be cleaned with a cotton wipe and ear cleaner made especially for dog's ears.

Brush your German Shorthaired Pointer thoroughly to get rid of any dead hair and debris before wetting his coat. Make certain that your dog has a good non-slip surface to stand on. Begin by wetting the dog's coat. A shower or hose attachment is necessary for thoroughly wetting and rinsing the coat. Check the water temperature to make sure that it is neither too hot nor too cold.

Next, apply shampoo to the dog's coat and work it into a

Right: A grooming glove with bristles makes it easy for you to give your GSP a once-over, and many dogs enjoy the feel of being brushed with such a tool.

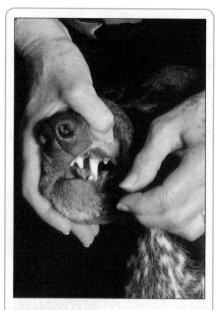

DEADLY DECAY
Did you know that periodontal disease (a condition of the bone and gums surrounding a tooth) can be fatal? Having your dog's teeth and mouth checked yearly can prevent it.

opportunity to check the skin for any bumps, bites or other abnormalities. Do not neglect any area of the body—get all of the hard-to-reach places.

Once the dog has been thoroughly shampooed, he requires an equally thorough rinsing. Shampoo left in the coat can be irritating to the skin. Protect his eyes from the shampoo by shielding them with your hand and directing the flow of water in the opposite direction. You should also avoid getting water in the ear canal. Be prepared for your GSP to shake out his coat—you might want to stand back, but make sure you have a hold on the dog to keep him from running through the house. Have a heavy towel on hand to dry his coat.

good lather. You should purchase a shampoo that is made for dogs. Do not use a product made for human hair; products for humans are too strong for dogs and will strip a dog's coat of the protective oils that make him water-resistant. Wash the head last; you do not want shampoo to drip into the dog's eyes while you are washing the rest of his body. Work the shampoo all the way down to the skin. You can use this

Specially made nail clippers for dogs will help make your GSP's pedicures easier.

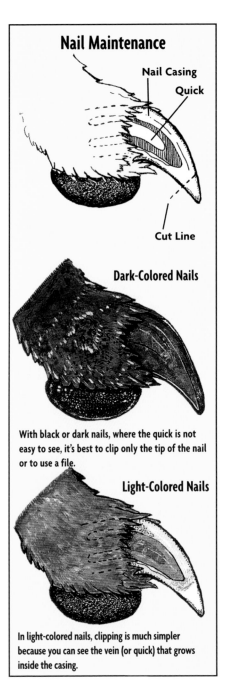

Nail Maintenance

Nail Casing

Quick

Cut Line

Dark-Colored Nails

With black or dark nails, where the quick is not easy to see, it's best to clip only the tip of the nail or to use a file.

Light-Colored Nails

In light-colored nails, clipping is much simpler because you can see the vein (or quick) that grows inside the casing.

PEDICURE TIP
A dog that spends a lot of time outside on a hard surface, such as cement or pavement, will have his nails naturally worn down and may not need to have them trimmed as often, except maybe in the colder months when he is not outside as much. Regardless, it is best to get your dog accustomed to the nail-trimming procedure at an early age so that he is used to it. Some dogs are especially sensitive about having their feet touched, but if a dog has experienced it since puppyhood, it should not bother him.

EAR CLEANING

Check the ears for waxy build-up, mites or other problems that commonly affect the drop-eared breeds. The ears should be kept clean with a cotton ball and ear cleaner made especially for dogs. Be on the lookout for any signs of infection or ear-mite infestation. If your German Shorthaired Pointer has been shaking his head or scratching at his ears, this usually indicates a problem. If his ears have an unusual odor, this is a sure sign of mite infestation or infection, and a signal to have his ears checked by the vet.

NAIL CLIPPING

Your German Shorthaired Pointer should be accustomed to having his nails trimmed at an early age, since it will be a part of your maintenance routine throughout his life. Not only does it look nicer, but long nails can scratch someone unintentionally. Also, a long nail has a better chance of ripping and bleeding, or of causing the feet to spread. A good rule of thumb is that if you can hear your dog's nails' clicking on the floor when he walks, his nails are too long.

Before you start cutting, make sure you can identify the "quick" in each nail. The quick is a blood vessel that runs through the center of each nail and grows rather close to the end. It will bleed if accidentally cut, which will be quite painful for the dog as it contains nerve endings. Keep some type of clotting agent on hand, such as a styptic pencil or styptic powder (the type used for shaving). This will stop the bleeding quickly when applied to the end of the cut nail. Do not panic if you cut the quick, just stop the bleeding and talk soothingly to your dog. Once he has calmed down, move on to the next nail. It is better to clip a little at a time, particularly with black-nailed dogs.

Hold your pup steady as you begin trimming his nails; you do not want him to make any sudden movements or run away. Talk to him soothingly and stroke him as you clip. Holding his foot in your hand, simply take off the end of each nail in

LET THE SUN SHINE

Your dog needs daily sunshine for the same reason people do. Pets kept inside homes with curtains drawn against the sun suffer from "SAD" (Seasonal Affected Disorder) to the same degree as humans. We now know that sunlight must enter the iris and thus progress to the pineal gland to regulate the body's hormonal system. When we live and work in artificial light, both circadian rhythms and hormone balances are disturbed.

one quick clip. You can purchase nail clippers that are specially made for dogs; you can probably find them wherever you buy pet or supplies.

TRAVELING WITH YOUR DOG

CAR TRAVEL

You should accustom your GSP to riding in a car at an early age. You may or may not take him in the car often, but at the very least he will need to go to the vet and you do not want these trips to be traumatic for the dog or troublesome for you. The safest way for a dog to ride in the car is in his crate. If he uses a crate in the house, you can use the same crate for travel.

Put the pup in the crate and see how he reacts. If he seems uneasy, you can have a passenger hold him on his lap while you drive. Another option is a specially made safety harness for dogs, which straps the dog in much like a seat belt. Do not let the dog roam loose in the vehicle—this is very dangerous! If you should stop short, your dog can be thrown and injured. If the dog starts climbing on you and pestering you while you are driving, you will not be able to concentrate on the road. It is an unsafe situation for everyone.

For long trips, be prepared to stop to let the dog relieve himself. Take with you whatever

> **MOTION SICKNESS**
> *If life is a motorway...*your dog may not want to come along for the ride! Some dogs experience motion sickness in cars that leads to excessive salivation and even vomiting. In most cases, your dog will fare better in the familiar, safe confines of his crate. To desensitize your dog, try going on several short jaunts before trying a long trip. If your dog experiences distress when riding in the vehicle, drive with him only when absolutely necessary, and do not feed him or give him water before you go.

you need to clean up after him, including some paper towels and some old bath towels for use should he have a potty accident in the car or suffer from motion sickness.

AIR TRAVEL

Contact your chosen airline before proceeding with your travel plans that include your German Shorthaired Pointer. The dog will be required to travel in a fiberglass crate and you should always check in advance with the airline regarding specific requirements for the crate's size, type and labeling. To help put the dog at ease, give him one of his favorite toys in the crate. Do not feed the dog for several hours prior to checking in so that you minimize his need to relieve himself. However, some airlines require that the dog must be fed within a certain time frame of arriving at the airport, in which case a light meal is best. For long trips, you will have to attach food and water bowls to the dog's crate so that airline employees can tend to him between legs of the trip.

Make sure that your dog is properly identified and that your contact information appears on his ID tags and on his crate. Your GSP will travel in a different area of the plane than the human passengers, so every rule must be strictly followed to prevent the risk of getting separated from your dog.

VACATIONS AND BOARDING

So you want to take a family vacation—and you want to include *all* members of the family. You would probably make arrangements for accommodation ahead of time anyway,

Always bring along water for your GSP whenever you are exercising him or traveling together.

but this is especially important when traveling with a dog. You do not want to make an overnight stop at the only place around for miles and find out that they do not allow dogs. Also, you do not want to reserve a room for your family without confirming that you are traveling with a dog because, if it is against their policy, you may not have a place to stay.

Alternatively, if you are traveling and choose not to bring your GSP, you will have to make arrangements for him while you are away. Some options are to take him to a neighbor's house to stay while you are gone, to have a trusted neighbor stop by often or stay at your house or to bring your dog to a reputable boarding kennel or possibly your vet's. If you choose to board him at a kennel, you should visit in advance to see the facilities provided, how

---

TRAVEL TIP

Never leave your dog alone in the car. In hot weather, your dog can die from the high temperature inside a closed vehicle; even a car parked in the shade can heat up very quickly. Leaving the window open is dangerous as well since the dog can hurt himself trying to get out.

Visit some local boarding kennels and select a suitable kennel before you actually need it. Ensure that it is clean, professionally run and large enough to comfortably accommodate your GSP.

clean they are and where the dogs are kept. Talk to some of the employees and see how they treat the dogs—do they spend time with the dogs, play with them, exercise them, etc.? Also find out the kennel's policy on vaccinations and what they

require. This is for all of the dogs' safety, since when dogs are kept together, there is a greater risk of diseases being passed from dog to dog.

Every dog should have his identification tags attached to his everyday collar at all times.

IDENTIFICATION
Your GSP is your valued companion and friend. That is why you always keep a close eye on him and you have made sure that he cannot escape from the yard or wriggle out of his collar and run away from you. However, accidents can happen and there may come a time when your dog unexpectedly gets separated from you. If this unfortunate event should occur, the first thing on your mind will

be finding him. Proper identification, including an ID tag and possibly a tattoo and/or a microchip, will increase the chances of his being returned to you safely and quickly.

IDENTIFICATION OPTIONS

As puppies become more and more expensive, especially those puppies of high quality for showing and/or breeding, they have a greater chance of being stolen. The usual collar dog tag is, of course, easily removed. But there are two permanent techniques that have become widely used for identification.

The puppy microchip implantation involves the injection of a small microchip, about the size of a corn kernel, under the skin of the dog. If your dog shows up at a clinic or shelter, or is offered for resale under less-than-savory circumstances, it can be positively identified by the microchip. The microchip is scanned, and a registry quickly identifies you as the owner.

Tattooing is done on various parts of the dog, from his belly to his cheeks. The number tattooed can be your telephone number or any other number that you can easily memorize. When professional dog thieves see a tattooed dog, they usually lose interest. For the safety of our dogs, no laboratory facility or dog broker will accept a tattooed dog as stock. Both microchipping and tattooing can be done at your local veterinary clinic.

ID tags tell a person who finds a lost dog that he is a pet, not a stray. The tags give important contact information to help ensure the dog's return to his owner.

GERMAN SHORTHAIRED POINTER

Living with an untrained dog is a lot like owning a piano that you do not know how to play—it is a nice object to look at, but it does not do much more than that to bring you pleasure. Now try taking piano lessons, and suddenly the piano comes alive and brings forth magical sounds and rhythms that set your heart singing and your body swaying.

The same is true with your German Shorthaired Pointer. Any dog is a big responsibility and if not trained sensibly may develop unacceptable behavior that

Housebreaking is an important and necessary part of your dog's training.

> **OBEDIENCE SCHOOL**
> Taking your dog to an obedience school may be the best investment in time and money you can ever make. You will enjoy the benefits for the lifetime of your dog and you will have the opportunity to meet people who have similar expectations for companion dogs. Plus, your dog will have the opportunity to socialize with other dogs.

annoys you or could even cause family friction.

To train your German Short-haired Pointer, you may like to enroll in an obedience class. Teach him good manners as you learn how and why he behaves the way he does. Find out how to communicate with your dog and how to recognize and understand his communications with you. Suddenly the dog takes on a new role in your life—he is clever, interesting, well-behaved and fun to be with. He demonstrates his bond of devotion to you daily. In other words, your German Shorthaired Pointer does

wonders for your ego because he constantly reminds you that you are not only his leader, you are his hero!

Those involved with teaching dog obedience and counseling owners about their dogs' behavior have discovered some interesting facts about dog ownership. For example, training dogs when they are puppies results in the highest rate of success in developing well-mannered and well-adjusted adult dogs. Training an older dog, from six months to six years of age, can produce almost equal results, providing that the owner accepts the dog's slower rate of learning capability and is willing to work patiently to help the dog succeed at developing to his fullest potential. Unfortunately, many owners of untrained adult dogs lack the patience factor, so they do not persist until their dogs are successful at learning particular behaviors.

Training a puppy aged 10 to 16 weeks (20 weeks at the most) is like working with a dry sponge in a pool of water. The pup soaks up whatever you show him and constantly looks for more things to do and learn. At this early age, his body is not yet producing hormones, and therein lies the reason for such a high rate of success. Without hormones, he is focused on his owners and not particularly

REAP THE REWARDS
If you start with a normal, healthy dog and give him time, patience and some carefully executed lessons, you will reap the rewards of that training for the life of the dog. And what a life it will be! The two of you will find immeasurable pleasure in the companionship you have built together with love, respect and understanding.

interested in investigating other places, dogs, people, etc. You are his leader: his provider of food, water, shelter and security. He latches onto you and wants to stay close. He will usually follow you from room to room, will not let you out of his sight when you are outdoors with him and will respond in like manner to the people and animals you encounter. If you greet a friend warmly, he will be happy to greet the person as well. If, however, you are hesitant or anxious about the approach of a stranger, he will respond accordingly.

Once the puppy begins to produce hormones, his natural curiosity emerges and he begins to investigate the world around him. It is at this time when you may notice that the untrained dog begins to wander away from you and even ignore your commands to stay close. When this behavior becomes a problem, the owner has two choices: get rid of the dog or train him. It

The eager-to-please GSP usually makes an attentive student, but it never hurts to have a treat on hand to keep him focused on the lesson.

> **CALM DOWN**
> Dogs will do anything for your attention. If you reward the dog when he is calm and attentive, you will develop a well-mannered dog. If, on the other hand, you greet your dog excitedly and encourage him to wrestle with you, the dog will greet you the same way and you will have a hyperactive dog on your hands.

is strongly urged that you choose the latter option.

There are usually classes within a reasonable distance from your home, but you can also do a lot to train your dog yourself. Sometimes there are classes available but the tuition is too costly. Whatever the circumstances, the solution to training your GSP without formal lessons lies within the pages of this book.

This chapter is devoted to helping you train your German Shorthaired Pointer at home. If the recommended procedures are followed faithfully, you may expect positive results that will prove rewarding both to you and your dog.

Whether your new charge is a puppy or a mature adult, the methods of teaching and the techniques we use in training basic behaviors are the same. After all, no dog, whether puppy or adult, likes harsh or inhu-

mane methods. All creatures, however, respond favorably to gentle motivational methods and sincere praise and encouragement. Now let us get started.

HOUSEBREAKING

You can train a puppy to relieve himself wherever you choose, but this must be somewhere suitable. You should bear in mind from the outset that when your puppy is old enough to go out in public places, any canine deposits must be removed at

THINK BEFORE YOU BARK

Dogs are sensitive to their masters' moods and emotions. Use your voice wisely when communicating with your dog. Never raise your voice at your dog unless you are trying to correct him. "Barking" at your dog can become as meaningless as "dogspeak" is to you.

once. You will always have to carry with you a small plastic bag or "poop-scoop."

Outdoor training includes such surfaces as grass, soil and cement. Indoor training usually means training your dog to newspaper, which is not a very viable option with a dog the size of the GSP.

When deciding on the surface and location that you will want your German Short-

Having a well-trained dog makes everything you do together easier, such as routine tasks like grooming.

HONOR AND OBEY

Dogs are the most honorable animals in existence. They consider another species (humans) as their own. They interface with you. You are their leader. Puppies perceive children to be on their level; their actions around small children are different from their behavior around their adult masters.

haired Pointer to use, be sure it is going to be permanent. Training your dog to grass and then changing your mind two months later is extremely difficult for both dog and owner.

Next, choose the command you will use each and every time you want your puppy to void. "Hurry up" and "Let's go" are examples of commands commonly used by dog owners. Get in the habit of giving the puppy your chosen relief command

before you take him out. That way, when he becomes an adult, you will be able to determine if he wants to go out when you ask him. A confirmation will be signs of interest such as wagging his tail, watching you intently, going to the door, etc.

PUPPY'S NEEDS

The puppy needs to relieve himself after play periods, after each meal, after he has been sleeping and at any time he indicates that he is looking for a place to urinate or defecate. The urinary and intestinal tract muscles of very young puppies are not fully developed. Therefore, like human babies, puppies need to relieve themselves frequently.

Take your puppy out often—every hour for an eight-week-old, for example, and always immediately after he has been sleeping and eating. The older the puppy, the less often he will need to relieve himself. Finally, as a mature healthy adult, he will require only three to five relief trips per day.

HOUSING

Since the types of housing and control you provide for your puppy have a direct relationship on the success of housebreaking, we consider the various aspects of both before we begin training.

Taking a new puppy home and turning him loose in your

CANINE DEVELOPMENT SCHEDULE

It is important to understand how and at what age a puppy develops into adulthood. If you are a puppy owner, consult the following Canine Development Schedule to determine the stage of development your puppy is currently experiencing. This knowledge will help you as you work with the puppy in the weeks and months ahead.

Period	Age	Characteristics
FIRST TO THIRD	BIRTH TO SEVEN WEEKS	Puppy needs food, sleep and warmth, and responds to simple and gentle touching. Needs mother for security and disciplining. Needs littermates for learning and interacting with other dogs. Pup learns to function within a pack and learns pack order of dominance. Begin socializing with adults and children for short periods. Begins to become aware of his environment.
FOURTH	EIGHT TO TWELVE WEEKS	Brain is fully developed. Needs socializing with outside world. Remove from mother and littermates. Needs to change from canine pack to human pack. Human dominance necessary. Fear period occurs between 8 and 16 weeks. Avoid fright and pain.
FIFTH	THIRTEEN TO SIXTEEN WEEKS	Training and formal obedience should begin. Less association with other dogs, more with people, places, situations. Period will pass easily if you remember this is pup's change-to-adolescence time. Be firm and fair. Flight instinct prominent. Permissiveness and over-disciplining can do permanent damage. Praise for good behavior.
JUVENILE	FOUR TO EIGHT MONTHS	Another fear period about 7 to 8 months of age. It passes quickly, but be cautious of fright and pain. Sexual maturity reached. Dominant traits established. Dog should understand sit, down, come and stay by now.

NOTE: THESE ARE APPROXIMATE TIME FRAMES. ALLOW FOR INDIVIDUAL DIFFERENCES IN PUPPIES.

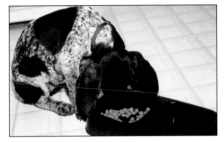

house can be compared to turning a child loose in a sports arena and telling the child that the place is all his! The sheer enormity of the place would be too much for him to handle.

Instead, offer the puppy clearly defined areas where he can play, sleep, eat and live. A room of the house where the family gathers is the most obvious choice. Puppies are social animals and need to feel a part of the pack right from the start. Hearing your voice, watching you while you are doing things and smelling you nearby are all positive reinforcers that he is now a member of your pack. Usually a family room, the kitchen or a nearby adjoining breakfast area is ideal for providing safety and security for both

puppy and owner.

Within that room there should be a smaller area that the puppy can call his own. An alcove, a wire or fiberglass dog crate or a fenced (not boarded!) corner from which he can view the activities of his new family will be fine. The size of the area or crate is the key factor here. The area must be large enough for the puppy to lie down and stretch out as well as stand up without rubbing his head on the top, yet small enough so that he cannot relieve himself at one end and sleep at the other without coming into contact with his droppings before he is fully trained to relieve himself outside. Dogs are, by nature, clean animals and will not remain close to their relief areas unless forced to do so. In those cases, they then become dirty dogs and usually remain that way for life.

The designated area should contain clean bedding and a toy. Once the puppy is housebroken reliably, water should always be available in his area.

PAPER CAPER

Never line your pup's sleeping area with newspaper. Puppy litters are usually raised on newspaper and, once in your home, the puppy will immediately associate newspaper with voiding. Never put newspaper on any floor while house-training, as this will only confuse the puppy. Finally, restrict water intake after evening meals. Offer a few licks at a time—never let a puppy (or an adult) gulp water after meals.

COMMAND STANCE
Stand up straight and authoritatively when giving your dog commands. Do not issue commands when lying on the floor or lying on your back on the sofa. If you are on your hands and knees when you give a command, your dog will think you are positioning yourself to play.

shorted wire can start a fire in the house. If the puppy chews on the arm of the chair when he is alone, you will probably discipline him angrily when you get home. Thus, he makes the association that your coming home means he is going to be punished. (He will not remember chewing the chair and is incapable of

CONTROL

By *control*, we mean helping the puppy to create a lifestyle pattern that will be compatible to that of his human pack (*you!*). Just as we guide little children to learn our way of life, we must show the puppy when it is time to play, eat, sleep, exercise and even entertain himself.

Your puppy should always sleep in his crate. He should also learn that, during times of household confusion and excessive human activity such as at breakfast when family members are preparing for the day, he can play by himself in relative safety and comfort in his designated area. Each time you leave the puppy alone, he should understand exactly where he is to stay.

Puppies are chewers. They cannot tell the difference between safe chew toys and lamp cords, television wires, shoes, table legs, etc. Chewing into a television wire, for example, can be fatal to the puppy, while a

A well-trained GSP is a pleasure to own, as you will enjoy spending time with your well-behaved, active canine companion.

making the association of the discipline with his naughty deed.) Having a designated area or crate for the puppy prevents these dangerous and/or destructive behaviors from happening.

Times of excitement, such as visits, family parties, etc., can be fun for the puppy, providing he can view the activities from the security of his designated area. He is not underfoot and he is not being fed all sorts of tidbits that will probably cause him stomach distress, yet he still feels a part of the fun.

TAKE THE LEAD
Do not carry your dog to his relief area. Lead him there on a leash or, better yet, encourage him to follow you to the spot. If you start carrying him to his spot, you might end up doing this routine forever and your dog will have the satisfaction of having trained *you.*

House-training and leash-training go hand in hand. You will have no success leading a dog to his relief area unless you have already accustomed the dog to the leash.

SCHEDULE

A puppy should be taken to his relief area each time he is released from his designated area, after meals, after play sessions and when he first awakens in the morning (at age eight weeks, this can mean 5 a.m.!). The puppy will indicate that he's ready "to go" by circling or sniffing busily—do not misinterpret these signs. For a puppy less than ten weeks of age, a routine of taking him out every hour is necessary. As the puppy grows, he will be able to wait for longer periods of time.

Keep trips to his relief area short. Stay no more than five or six minutes and then return to the house. If he goes during that time, praise him lavishly and take him indoors immediately. If he does not, but he has an accident when you go back indoors, pick him up immediately, say "No! No!" and return to his relief area. Wait a few minutes, then return to the house again. Never hit a puppy or put his face in his urine or excrement when he has had an accident!

Once indoors, put the puppy in his crate until you have had time to clean up his accident. Then release him to the family area and watch him more closely than before. Chances are, his accident was a result of your not picking up his signal or waiting too long before offering him the

HOW MANY TIMES A DAY?

AGE	RELIEF TRIPS
To 14 weeks	10
14–22 weeks	8
22–32 weeks	6
Adulthood	4
(dog stops growing)	

These are estimates, of course, but they are a guide to the *minimum* number of opportunities a dog should have each day to relieve himself.

opportunity to relieve himself. Never hold a grudge against the puppy for accidents.

Let the puppy learn that going outdoors means it is time to relieve himself, not to play. Once trained, he will be able to play indoors and out and still differentiate between the times for play versus the times for relief.

Help him develop regular hours for naps, being alone, playing by himself and just resting, all in his crate. Encourage him to entertain himself while you are busy with your activities. Let him learn that having you near is comforting, but it is not your main purpose in life to provide him with your undivided attention.

Each time you put your puppy in his own area, use the same command, whatever suits best. Soon he will run to his crate or special area when he hears you say those words.

Crate training provides safety for you, the puppy and the home. It also provides the puppy with a feeling of security, and that helps the puppy achieve self-confidence and clean living and toileting habits.

THE SUCCESS METHOD
6 Steps to Successful Crate Training

1 Tell the puppy "Crate time!" and place him in the crate with a small treat (a piece of cheese or half of a biscuit). Let him stay in the crate for five minutes while you are in the same room. Then release him and praise lavishly. Never release him when he is fussing. Wait until he is quiet before you let him out.

2 Repeat Step 1 several times a day.

3 The next day, place the puppy in the crate as before. Let him stay there for ten minutes. Do this several times.

4 Continue building time in five-minute increments until the puppy stays in his crate for 30 minutes with you in the room. Always take him to his relief area after prolonged periods in his crate.

5 Now go back to Step 1 and let the puppy stay in his crate for five minutes, this time while you are out of the room.

6 Once again, build crate time in five-minute increments with you out of the room. When the puppy will stay willingly in his crate (he may even fall asleep!) for 30 minutes with you out of the room, he will be ready to stay in it for several hours at a time.

HOUSEBREAKING TIP

Most of all, be consistent. Always take your dog to the same location, always use the same command and always have the dog on lead when he is in his relief area, unless a fenced-in yard is available.

By following the Success Method, your puppy will be completely house-broken by the time his muscle and brain development reach maturity. Keep in mind that small breeds usually mature faster than large breeds, but all puppies should be trained by six months of age.

Remember that one of the primary ingredients in house-breaking your puppy is control. Regardless of your lifestyle, there will always be occasions when you will need to have a place where your dog can stay and be happy and safe. Crate training is the answer for now and in the future.

In conclusion, a few key elements are really all you need for a successful housebreaking method—consistency, frequency, praise, control and supervision. By following these procedures

A baby gate is useful for parti-tioning a room in which your pup can stay and be safe when you can't be there to supervise him.

LANGUAGE BARRIER

Dogs do not understand our language and have to rely on tone of voice more than just works or sound. They can be trained to react to a certain sound, at a certain volume. If you say "No, Oliver" in a very soft, pleasant voice, it will not have the same meaning as "No, Oliver!!" when you raise your voice. You should never use the dog's name during a reprimand, just the command "No! " You never want the dog to associate his name with a negative experience or reprimand.

with a normal, healthy puppy, you and the puppy will soon be past the stage of "accidents" and ready to move on to a full and rewarding life together.

ROLES OF DISCIPLINE, REWARD AND PUNISHMENT

Discipline, training one to act in accordance with rules, brings order to life. It is as simple as that. Without discipline, particularly in a group society, chaos reigns supreme and the group will eventually perish. Humans and canines are social animals and need some form of discipline in order to function effectively. They must procure food, reproduce to keep the species going and protect their home base and their young.

If there were no discipline in the lives of social animals, they would eventually die from starvation and/or predation by other stronger animals. In the case of domestic canines, dogs need discipline in their lives in order to understand how their pack (you and other family members) functions and how they must act in order to survive.

A large humane society in a highly populated area recently surveyed dog owners regarding their satisfaction with their relationships with their dogs. People who had trained their dogs were 75% more satisfied with their pets than those who had never trained their dogs.

Dr. Edward Thorndike, a noted psychologist, established *Thorndike's Theory of Learning*, which states that a behavior that results in a pleasant event tends to be repeated. Likewise, a behavior that results in an unpleasant event tends not to be repeated. It is this theory on which training methods are based today. For example, if you manipulate a dog to perform a specific behavior and reward him for doing it, he is likely to do it again because he enjoyed the end result.

Occasionally, punishment, a penalty inflicted for an offense, is necessary. The best type of punishment often comes from an outside source. For example, a child is told not to touch the stove because he may get burned. He disobeys and touches the stove. In doing so, he receives a burn. From that time on, he respects the heat of the stove and avoids contact with it. Therefore, a behavior that results in an unpleasant event tends not to be repeated.

A good example of a dog learning the hard way is the dog who chases the house cat. He is told many times to leave the cat alone, yet he persists in teasing the cat. Then, one day he begins chasing the cat but the cat turns and swipes a claw across the dog's face, leaving him with a painful gash on his nose. The final result is that the dog stops chasing the cat.

TRAINING EQUIPMENT

COLLAR AND LEASH

For a German Shorthaired Pointer, the collar and leash that you use for training must be one with which you are easily able to work, not too heavy for the dog and perfectly safe.

> **KEEP SMILING**
> Never train your dog, puppy or adult, when you are angry or in a sour mood. Dogs are very sensitive to human feelings, especially anger, and if your dog senses that you are angry or upset, he will connect your anger with his training and learn to resent or fear his training sessions.

TREATS

Have a bag of treats on hand. Something nutritious and easy to swallow works best. Use a soft treat, a chunk of cheese or a piece of cooked chicken rather than a dry biscuit. By the time the dog has finished chewing a dry treat, he will forget why he is being rewarded in the first place! Using food rewards will not teach a dog to beg at the table—the only way to teach a dog to beg at the table is to give him food from the table. In training, rewarding the dog with a

Careful introductions and your caring attitude toward all pets in the home will foster good relationships between the animals in a multi-pet household.

food treat will help him associate praise and the treats with learning new behaviors that obviously please his owner.

TRAINING BEGINS: ASK THE DOG A QUESTION

In order to teach your dog anything, you must first get his attention. After all, he cannot learn anything if he is looking away from you with his mind on something else.

To get your GSP's attention, ask him "School?" and immediately walk over to him and give him a treat as you tell him

The whole family should be involved in the GSP's training so that he learns to behave well no matter who issues a command.

"Good dog." Wait a minute or two and repeat the routine, this time with a treat in your hand as you approach within a foot of the dog. Do not go directly to him, but stop about a foot short of him and hold out the treat as you ask "School?" He will see you approaching with a treat in your hand and most likely begin walking toward you. As you meet, give him the treat and praise again.

The third time, ask the question, have a treat in your hand and walk only a short distance toward the dog so that he must walk almost all the way to you. As he reaches you, give him the treat and praise again.

By this time, the dog will probably be getting the idea that if he pays attention to you, especially when you ask that question, it will pay off in treats and enjoyable activities for him. In other words, he learns that "school" means doing great things with you that are fun and result in positive attention for him.

Remember that the dog does not understand your verbal language; he only recognizes sounds. Your question translates to a series of sounds for him, and those sounds become the signal to go to you and pay attention; if he does, he will get to interact with you plus receive treats and praise.

THE BASIC COMMANDS

TEACHING SIT

Now that you have the dog's attention, attach his leash and hold it in your left hand and a food treat in your right. Place your food hand at the dog's nose and let him lick the treat but not take it from you. Say "Sit" and slowly raise your food hand from in front of the dog's nose up over his head so that he is looking at the ceiling. As he bends his head upward, he will have to bend his knees to maintain his balance. As he bends his knees, he will assume a sit position. At that point, release the food treat and praise lavishly with comments

Getting your dog's attention with a treat is guaranteed. Produce a tasty tidbit and watch your student snap to attention.

such as "Good dog! Good sit!," etc. Remember to always praise enthusiastically, because dogs relish verbal praise from their owners and feel so proud of themselves whenever they accomplish a behavior.

You will not use food forever in getting the dog to obey your commands. Food is only used to teach new behaviors, and once the dog knows what you want when you give a specific command, you will wean him off the food treats but still maintain the verbal praise. After all, you will always have your voice with you, and there will be many times when you have no food rewards but expect the dog to obey.

TEACHING DOWN

Teaching the down exercise is easy when you understand how the dog perceives the down posi-

---

PRACTICE MAKES PERFECT!

• Have training lessons with your dog every day in several short segments—three to five times a day for a few minutes at a time is ideal.
• Do not have long practice sessions. The dog will become easily bored.
• Never practice when you are tired, ill, worried or in an otherwise negative mood. This will transmit to the dog and may have an adverse effect on his performance.

Think fun, short and above all *positive!* End each session on a high note, rather than a failed exercise, and make sure to give a lot of praise. Enjoy the training and help your dog enjoy it, too.

The sit exercise is probably the most simple of the commands to teach your dog. Other exercises, like stay and heel, build from the sit.

THE GOLDEN RULE
The golden rule of dog training is simple. For each "question" (command), there is only one correct answer (reaction). One command = one reaction. Keep practicing the command until the dog reacts correctly without hesitating. Be repetitive but not monotonous. Dogs get bored just as people do!

tion, and it is very difficult when you do not. Dogs perceive the down position as a submissive one; therefore, teaching the down exercise using a forceful method can sometimes make the dog develop such a fear of the down that he either runs away when you say "Down" or he attempts to snap at the person who tries to force him down.

Have the dog sit close alongside your left leg, facing in the same direction as you are. Hold the leash in your left hand and a food treat in your right. Now place your left hand lightly on the top of the dog's shoulders where they meet above the spinal cord. Do not push down on the dog's shoulders; simply rest your left hand there so you can guide the dog to lie down close to your left leg rather than to swing away from your side when he drops.

Now place the food hand at the dog's nose, say "Down" very softly (almost a whisper) and slowly lower the food hand to the dog's front feet. When the food hand reaches the floor, begin moving it forward along the floor in front of the dog. Keep talking softly to the dog, saying things like, "Do you want this treat? You can do this, good dog." Your reassuring tone of voice will help calm the dog as he tries to follow the food hand in order to get the treat.

When the dog's elbows touch the floor, release the food and praise softly. Try to get the dog to maintain that down position for several seconds before you let him sit up again. The goal here is to get the dog to settle down and not feel threatened in the down position.

TEACHING STAY

It is easy to teach the dog to stay in either a sit or a down position. Again, we use food and praise during the teaching process as we help the dog to understand exactly what it is that we are expecting him to do.

To teach the sit/stay, start with the dog sitting on your left side as before and hold the leash in your left hand. Have a food

The stay command is taught using a combination of verbal commands and hand signals.

DOUBLE JEOPARDY

A dog in jeopardy never lies down. He stays alert on his feet because instinct tells him that he may have to run away or fight for his survival. Therefore, if a dog feels threatened or anxious, he will not lie down. Consequently, it is important to keep the dog calm and relaxed as he learns the down exercise.

FEAR AGGRESSION

Fear in a grown dog is often the result of improper or incomplete socialization as a pup, or it can be the result of a traumatic experience he suffered when young. For example, pups who are subjected to physical abuse during training commonly end up with behavioral problems as adults. One common result of abuse is fear aggression, in which a dog will lash out, bare his teeth, snarl and finally bite someone by whom he feels threatened. For example, your daughter may be playing with the dog one afternoon. As they play hide-and-seek, she backs the dog into a corner and, as she attempts to tease him playfully, he bites her hand. Examine the cause of this behavior. Did your daughter ever hit the dog? Did someone who resembles your daughter hit or scream at the dog?

Fortunately, fear aggression is relatively easy to correct. Have your daughter engage in only positive activities with the dog, such as feeding, petting and walking. She should not give any corrections or negative feedback. If the dog still growls or cowers away from her, allow someone else to accompany them. After approximately one week, the dog should feel that he can rely on her for many positive things, and he will also be prevented from reacting fearfully towards anyone who might resemble her.

treat in your right hand and place your food hand at the dog's nose. Say "Stay" and step out on your right foot to stand directly in front of the dog, toe to toe, as he licks and nibbles the treat. Be sure to keep his head facing upward to maintain the sit position. Count to five and then swing around to stand next to the dog again with him on your left. As soon as you get back to the original position, release the food and praise lavishly.

To teach the down/stay, do the down as previously described. As soon as the dog lies down, say "Stay" and step out on your right foot just as you did in the sit/stay. Count to five and then return to stand beside the dog with him on your left side. Release the treat and praise as always.

Within a week or ten days, you can begin to add a bit of distance between you and your dog when you leave him. When you do, use your left hand open with the palm facing the dog as a stay signal, much the same as the hand signal a police officer uses to stop traffic at an intersection. Hold the food treat in your right hand as before, but this time the food is not touching the dog's nose. He will watch the food hand and quickly learn that he is going to get that treat as soon as you return to his side.

When you can stand 3 feet

away from your dog for 30 seconds, you can then begin building time and distance in both stays. Eventually, the dog can be expected to remain in the stay position for prolonged periods of time until you return to him or call him to you. Always praise lavishly when he stays.

TEACHING COME

If you make teaching "come" an exciting experience, you should never have a "student" that does not love the game or that fails to

CONSISTENCY PAYS OFF

Dogs need consistency in their feeding schedule, exercise and relief visits, and in the verbal commands you use. If you use "Stay" on Monday and "Stay here, please" on Tuesday, you will confuse your dog. Don't demand perfect behavior during training sessions and then let him have the run of the house the rest of the day. Above all, lavish praise on your pet consistently every time he does something right. The more he feels he is pleasing you, the more willing he will be to learn.

Puppies need to be puppies! Remember to take frequent breaks from training to give your pup some play and fun time with you.

come when called. The secret, it seems, is never to teach the word "come."

At times when an owner most wants his dog to come when called, the owner is likely to be upset or anxious and he allows these feelings to come through in the tone of his voice when he calls his dog. Hearing that desperation in his owner's voice, the dog fears the results of going to him and therefore either disobeys outright or runs in the opposite direction. The secret, therefore, is to teach the dog a game and, when you want him to come to you, simply play the

More than one dog means more effort in training and your ability to control them. You must ensure that the dogs behave well with each other, walk politely on leash and respond reliably to basic commands.

> ### "COME" ... BACK
> Never call your dog to come to you for a correction or scold him when he reaches you. That is the quickest way to turn a come command into "Go away fast!" Dogs think only in the present tense, and your dog will connect the scolding with coming to you, not with the misbehavior of a few moments earlier.

game. It is practically a no-fail solution!

To begin, have several members of your family take a few food treats and each go into a different room in the house. Take turns calling the dog, and each person should celebrate the dog's finding him with a treat and lots of happy praise. When a person calls the dog, he is actually inviting the dog to find him and get a treat as a reward for "winning."

A few turns of the "Where are you?" game and the dog will understand that everyone is playing the game and that each person has a big celebration awaiting the dog's success at locating him. Once the dog learns to love the game, simply calling out "Where are you?" will bring him running from wherever he is when he hears that all-important question.

The come command is recognized as one of the most important things to teach a dog, but there are trainers who work with thousands of dogs and never teach the actual word "come." Yet these dogs will race to respond to a person who uses the dog's name followed by "Where are you?" For example, a woman has a 12-year-old companion dog who went blind, but who never fails to locate her owner when asked, "Where are you?"

Children, in particular, love to play this game with their dogs. Children can hide in smaller places like a shower stall or bathtub, behind a bed or under a table. The dog needs to work a little bit harder to find these hiding places, but, when he does, he loves to celebrate with a treat and a tussle with a favorite youngster.

TEACHING HEEL

Heeling means that the dog walks beside the owner without pulling. It takes time and patience on the owner's part to succeed at teaching the dog that he (the owner) will not proceed unless the dog is walking calmly beside him. Pulling out ahead on the leash is definitely not acceptable.

Begin by holding the leash in your left hand as the dog sits beside your left leg. Move the loop end of the leash to your right hand, but keep your left hand short on the leash so that it

TUG OF WALK?
If you begin teaching the heel by taking long walks and letting the dog pull you along, he misinterprets this action as an acceptable form of taking a walk. When you pull back on the leash to counteract his pulling, he reads that tug as a signal to pull even harder!

keeps the dog in close next to you.

Say "Heel" and step forward on your left foot. Keep the dog close to you and take three steps. Stop and have the dog sit next to you in what we now call the heel position. Praise verbally, but do not touch the dog. Hesitate a moment and begin again with

Whether a leisurely stroll or brisk jog, heeling means that your GSP stays in step with you at the pace you set.

Whether a leisurely stroll or brisk jog, heeling means that your GSP stays in step with you at the pace you set.

"Heel," taking three steps and stopping, at which point the dog is told to sit again.

Your goal here is to have the dog walk those three steps without pulling on the leash. Once he will walk calmly beside you for three steps without pulling, increase the number of steps you take to five. When he will walk politely beside you while you take five steps, you can increase the length of your walk to ten steps. Keep increasing the length of your stroll until the dog will walk quietly beside you without pulling as long as you want him to heel. When you stop heeling, indicate to the dog that the exercise is over by verbally praising as you pet him and say, "OK, good dog." The "OK" is used as a release word, meaning that the exercise is finished and the dog

is free to relax.

If you are dealing with a dog who insists on pulling you around, simply "put on your brakes" and stand your ground until the dog realizes that the two of you are not going anywhere until he is beside you and moving at your pace, not his. It may take some time just standing there to convince the dog that you are the leader and you will be the one to decide on the direction and speed of your travel.

Each time the dog looks up at you or slows down to give a slack leash between the two of you, quietly praise him and say, "Good heel. Good dog." Eventually, the dog will begin to respond and within a few days he will be walking politely beside you without pulling on the leash. At first, the training sessions should be kept short and very positive; soon the dog will be able to walk nicely with you for increasingly longer distances. Remember also to give

> **HEELING WELL**
> Teach your dog to heel in an enclosed area. Once you think the dog will obey reliably and you want to attempt advanced obedience exercises such as off-leash heeling, test him in a fenced-in area so he cannot run away.

the dog free time and the opportunity to run and play when you have finished heel practice.

WEANING OFF FOOD IN TRAINING

Food is used in training new behaviors. Once the dog understands what behavior goes with a specific command, it is time to start weaning him off the food treats. At first, give a treat after each exercise. Then, start to give a treat only after every other exercise. Mix up the times when you offer a food reward and the times when you only offer praise so that the dog will never know when he is going to receive both food and praise and when he is going to receive only praise. This is called a variable ratio reward system and it proves successful because there is always the chance that the owner will produce a treat, so the dog never stops trying for that reward. No matter what, *always* give verbal praise.

OBEDIENCE CLASSES

It is a good idea to enroll in an obedience class if one is available in your area. If yours is a show dog, preparatory classes for the show ring would be more appropriate. Many areas have dog clubs that offer basic obedience training as well as classes to prepare dog and handler for obedience competition. There are

HOW TO WEAN THE "TREAT HOG"

If you have trained your dog by rewarding him with a treat each time he performs a command, he may soon decide that without the treat, he won't sit, stay or come. The best way to fix this problem is to start asking your dog to do certain commands twice before being rewarded. Slowly increase the number of commands given before giving a treat. You can also reward your dog with things other than food, such as a favorite toy or some playtime with you. This has the added benefit of some exercise and quality fun time together.

also local dog trainers who offer similar classes.

At obedience trials, dogs can earn titles at various levels of competition. The beginning levels of competition include basic behaviors such as sit, down, heel, etc. The more advanced levels of competition include jumping, retrieving, scent discrimination and signal work. The advanced levels require a dog and owner to put a lot of time and effort into their training, and the titles that can be earned at these levels of competition are very prestigious.

OTHER ACTIVITIES FOR LIFE
Whether a dog is trained in the structured environment of a class or alone with his owner at home, there are many activities that can bring fun and rewards to both owner and dog once they have mastered basic control. Of course, with German Shorthaired Pointers, the hunt is the main allure for these talented gundogs, and owners are encouraged to pursue this endeavor with their dogs. GSPs excel not only as hunting companions but also as field trial competitors. If you are not inclined toward hunting or field trials, but still are enamored of the charms of the GSP, there are other activities that you can do with your dog.

Teaching the dog to help out around the home, in the garden or on the farm can provide great satisfaction to both dog and owner. In addition, the dog's help makes life a little easier for his owner and raises his stature as a valued companion to his family. It helps give the dog a purpose by occupying his mind and providing an outlet for his energy.

Backpacking is an exciting and healthy activity that the dog can be taught without assistance from more than his owner. The exercise of walking and climbing is good for man and dog alike, and the bond that they develop together is priceless. The rule for backpacking with any dog is never to allow the dog to carry more than one-sixth of his body weight.

If you are interested in participating in organized competition with your German Shorthaired Pointer, there are activities other than field trials and obedience trials in which you and your dog can become involved. Agility is a popular sport in which dogs run through an obstacle course that includes various jumps, tunnels and other exercises to test the dog's speed and coordination. The owners run beside their dogs to give commands and to guide the dogs through the course. Although competitive, the focus is on fun—it's fun to do, fun to watch and great exercise.

Agility is fun for the owner and the dog. There are usually training grounds in your area where you may take your dog for agility training.

Health Care of Your

GERMAN SHORTHAIRED POINTER

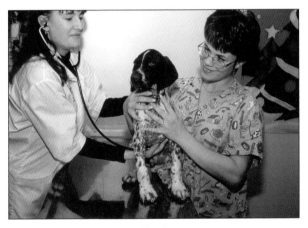

Your vet becomes your puppy's most important human contact—next to you, of course.

Dogs suffer from many of the same physical illnesses as people. They might even share many of the same psychological problems. Since people usually know more about human diseases than canine maladies, many of the terms used in this chapter will be familiar but not necessarily those used by veterinarians. We will use the term *x-ray*, instead of the more acceptable term *radiograph*. We will also use the familiar term *symptoms* even though dogs don't have symptoms, which are verbal descriptions of the patient's feelings; dogs have *clinical signs*.

Since dogs can't speak, we have to look for clinical signs...but we still use the term *symptoms* in this book.

As a general rule, medicine is *practiced*. That term is not arbitrary. Medicine is a constantly changing art as we learn more and more about genetics, electronic aids (like CAT scans and MRIs) and daily laboratory advances. There are many dog maladies, like canine hip dysplasia, which are not universally treated in the same manner. For example, some veterinarians opt for surgery more often than others do.

SELECTING A VETERINARIAN
Your selection of a veterinarian should be based upon personal

NEUTERING/SPAYING
Male dogs are neutered. The operation removes the testicles and requires that the dog be anesthetized. Recovery takes about one week. Females are spayed. This is major surgery and it usually takes a bitch two weeks to recover.

recommendation for his skills with small animals, especially dogs, and upon his convenience to your home. You want a vet who is close by because you might have emergencies or need to make multiple visits for treatments. You want a vet who has services that you might require such as tattooing and grooming, as well as sophisticated pet supplies and a good reputation for ability and responsiveness. There is nothing more frustrating than having to wait a day or more to get a response from your veterinarian.

All veterinarians are licensed and capable of dealing with routine medical issues and the promotion of health (for example, by vaccination). Most vets do routine surgery such as neutering,

Breakdown of Veterinary Income by Category

%	Category
2%	Dentistry
4%	Radiology
12%	Surgery
15%	Vaccinations
19%	Laboratory
23%	Examinations
25%	Medicines

A typical vet's income, categorized according to services performed. This survey dealt with small-animal (pets) practices.

> **PUPPY VACCINATIONS**
>
> Your veterinarian will probably recommend that your puppy be vaccinated before you take him outside. There are airborne diseases, parasite eggs in the grass and unexpected visits from other dogs that might be dangerous to your puppy's health.
>
> Vaccinations help prevent your new puppy from contracting diseases, but they do not cure them. Proper nutrition as well as parasite control keep your dog healthy and less susceptible to many dangerous diseases. Remember that your dog depends on you to ensure his well-being.

stitching up wounds and docking tails for those breeds in which such is required for show purposes. There are, however, many veterinary specialties that require further studies and internships. There are specialists in heart problems (veterinary cardiologists), skin problems (veterinary dermatologists), teeth and gum problems (veterinary dentists), eye problems (veterinary ophthalmologists) and x-rays (veterinary radiologists), as well as vets who have specialties in bones, muscles or certain organs. Your vet will refer your dog to a specialist in the appropriate field if the need arises.

When the problem affecting your dog is serious, it is not unusual or impudent to get another medical opinion, although it is courteous to advise the vets concerned about this. You might

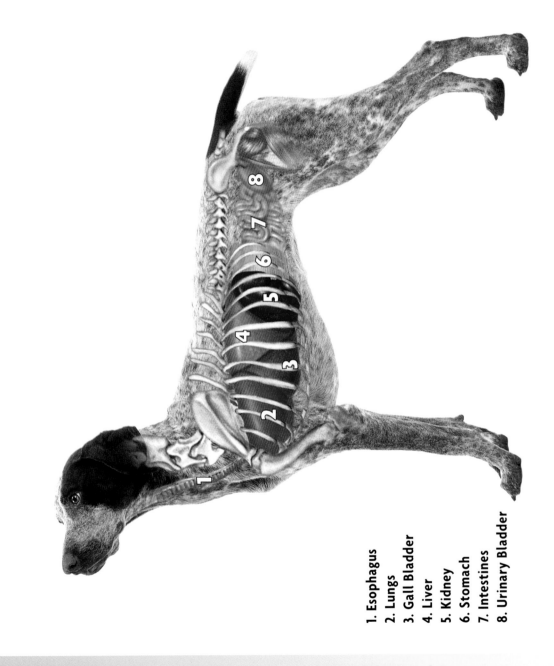

1. Esophagus
2. Lungs
3. Gall Bladder
4. Liver
5. Kidney
6. Stomach
7. Intestines
8. Urinary Bladder

Internal Organs of the German Shorthaired Pointer

also want to compare costs among several different vets. Sophisticated health care and veterinary services can be very costly, and cost may play a role in deciding which course of treatment to take.

PREVENTATIVE MEDICINE
It is much easier, less costly and more effective to practice preventative medicine than to fight bouts of illness and disease. Properly bred puppies come from parents who were selected based upon their genetic-disease profiles. Their mother should have been vaccinated, free of all internal and external parasites and properly nourished. For these reasons, a visit to the veterinarian who cared for the dam is recommended. The dam can pass on disease resistance to her puppies, which can last for eight to ten weeks. She can also pass on parasites and many infections. That's why it is helpful to know as much about the dam's health as possible.

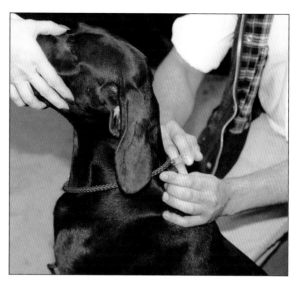

VACCINE ALLERGIES
Vaccines do not work all the time. Sometimes dogs are allergic to them and many times the antibodies, which are supposed to be stimulated by the vaccine, just are not produced. You should keep your dog in the veterinary clinic for an hour after he is vaccinated to be sure there are no allergic reactions.

VACCINATION SCHEDULING
Most vaccinations are given by injection and should only be done by a veterinarian. Both he and you should keep a record of the date of the injection, the identification of the vaccine and the amount given. Some vets give a first vaccination at eight weeks, but most dog breeders prefer the course not to commence until about ten weeks because of the risk of negating any antibodies passed on by the dam. The vaccination scheduling is usually based on a 15-day cycle. You must take your vet's advice regarding when to vaccinate, as this may differ according to the vaccine used.

Most vaccinations immunize your puppy against viruses. The usual vaccines contain immunizing doses of several different

Your vet will start your GSP on a vaccination schedule as a puppy and will oversee his booster-shot program as the dog gets older.

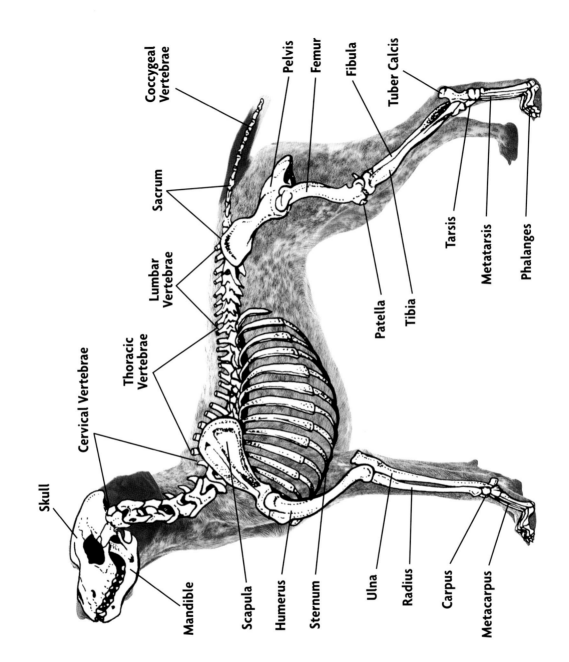

Coccygeal Vertebrae

Pelvis

Femur

Fibula

Tuber Calcis

Sacrum

Tarsis

Metatarsis

Phalanges

Lumbar Vertebrae

Patella

Tibia

Thoracic Vertebrae

Cervical Vertebrae

Skull

Mandible

Scapula

Humerus

Sternum

Ulna

Radius

Carpus

Metacarpus

Skeletal Structure of the German Shorthaired Pointer

viruses such as distemper, parvovirus, parainfluenza and hepatitis, although some veterinarians recommend separate vaccines for each disease. There are other vaccines available when the puppy is at risk. You should rely upon professional advice. This is especially true for the booster-shot program. Most vaccination programs require a booster when the puppy is a year old and once a year thereafter. In some cases, circumstances may require more or less frequent immunizations. Kennel cough, more formally known as tracheobronchitis, is treated with a vaccine that is sprayed into the dog's nostrils. Kennel cough is usually included in routine vaccination, but this is often not so effective as for other major diseases.

WEANING TO FIVE MONTHS OLD
Puppies should be weaned by the time they are about two months old. A puppy that remains for at least eight weeks with his mother and littermates usually adapts better to other dogs and people later in life.

Sometimes new owners have their puppy examined by a veterinarian immediately, which is a good idea unless the pup is overtired by the journey home. In that case, an appointment should be arranged for the next day. The puppy will have his teeth examined and have his skeletal confor-

KNOW WHEN TO POSTPONE A VACCINATION
While the visit to the vet is costly, it is never advisable to update a vaccination when visiting with a sick or pregnant dog. Vaccinations also should be avoided for all elderly dogs. If your dog is showing the signs of any illness or any medical condition, no matter how serious or mild, including skin irritations, do not vaccinate. Likewise, a lame dog should never be vaccinated; any dog undergoing surgery or on any immunosuppressant drugs should not be vaccinated until fully recovered.

mation and general health checked prior to certification by the vet. Puppies in certain breeds have problems with their kneecaps, cataracts and other eye problems, heart murmurs and undescended testicles. Your vet might also have training in temperament testing and evaluation. The vet will set up your pup's vaccination schedule at the first visit.

FIVE TO TWELVE MONTHS OF AGE
Unless you intend to breed or show your dog, neutering the puppy around six months of age is recommended. Discuss this with your veterinarian, as opinions vary regarding the best age at which to do this. Neutering and

Your GSP can't take himself to the vet—he looks up to you to keep up with his routine check-ups and to maintain his health at home between veterinary visits.

spaying have proven to be extremely beneficial to both male and female dogs, respectively. Besides eliminating the possibility of pregnancy, it inhibits (but does not prevent) breast cancer in bitches and prostate cancer in male dogs. Your vet can advise you on all aspects of the procedure.

Your veterinarian should provide your puppy with a thorough dental evaluation at six months of age, ascertaining whether all of the permanent teeth have erupted properly. A home dental-care regimen should be initiated at six months, including brushing weekly and providing good dental devices (such as nylon bones). Regular dental care promotes healthy teeth, fresh breath and a longer life.

OLDER THAN ONE YEAR
Once a year, your grown dog should visit the vet for an examination and vaccination boosters, if needed. Some vets recommend blood tests, thyroid level check and dental evaluation to accompany these annual visits. A thorough clinical evaluation by the vet can provide critical back-

HEALTH AND VACCINATION SCHEDULE

AGE IN WEEKS:	6TH	8TH	10TH	12TH	14TH	16TH	20-24TH	52ND
Worm Control	✔	✔	✔	✔	✔	✔	✔	
Neutering								✔
Heartworm		✔		✔		✔	✔	
Parvovirus	✔		✔		✔		✔	✔
Distemper		✔		✔		✔		✔
Hepatitis		✔		✔		✔		✔
Leptospirosis								✔
Parainfluenza	✔		✔		✔			✔
Dental Examination		✔					✔	✔
Complete Physical		✔					✔	✔
Coronavirus				✔			✔	✔
Kennel Cough	✔							
Hip Dysplasia								✔
Rabies							✔	

Vaccinations are not instantly effective. It takes about two weeks for the dog's immune system to develop antibodies. Most vaccinations require annual booster shots. Your vet should guide you in this regard.

DISEASE REFERENCE CHART

	What is it?	What causes it?	Symptoms
Leptospirosis	Severe disease that affects the internal organs; can be spread to people.	A bacterium, which is often carried by rodents, that enters through mucous membranes and spreads quickly throughout the body.	Range from fever, vomiting and loss of appetite in less severe cases to shock, irreversible kidney damage and possibly death in most severe cases.
Rabies	Potentially deadly virus that infects warm-blooded mammals.	Bite from a carrier of the virus, mainly wild animals.	1st stage: dog exhibits change in behavior, fear. 2nd stage: dog's behavior becomes more aggressive. 3rd stage: loss of coordination, trouble with bodily functions.
Parvovirus	Highly contagious virus, potentially deadly.	Ingestion of the virus, which is usually spread through the feces of infected dogs.	Most common: severe diarrhea. Also vomiting, fatigue, lack of appetite.
Kennel cough	Contagious respiratory infection.	Combination of types of bacteria and virus. Most common: *Bordetella bronchiseptica* bacteria and parainfluenza virus.	Chronic cough.
Distemper	Disease primarily affecting respiratory and nervous system.	Virus that is related to the human measles virus.	Mild symptoms such as fever, lack of appetite and mucus secretion progress to evidence of brain damage, "hard pad."
Hepatitis	Virus primarily affecting the liver.	Canine adenovirus type I (CAV-1). Enters system when dog breathes in particles.	Lesser symptoms include listlessness, diarrhea, vomiting. More severe symptoms include "blue-eye" (clumps of virus in eye).
Coronavirus	Virus resulting in digestive problems.	Virus is spread through infected dog's feces.	Stomach upset evidenced by lack of appetite, vomiting, diarrhea.

ground information for your dog. Blood tests are often performed at one year of age, and dental examinations around the third or fourth birthday. In the long run, quality preventative care for your pet can save money, teeth and lives.

SKIN PROBLEMS IN GERMAN SHORTHAIRED POINTERS

Veterinarians are consulted more frequently by dog owners for skin problems than for any other group of diseases or maladies. Dogs' skin is almost as sensitive as human skin and both suffer from almost the same ailments (though the occurrence of acne in most breeds of dog is rare!). For this reason, veterinary dermatology has developed into a specialty practiced by many veterinarians.

Since many skin problems have visual symptoms that are almost identical, it requires the skill of an experienced veterinary dermatologist to identify and cure many of the more severe skin

One of the most important reasons to visit your vet *prior* to bringing your puppy home is to ensure that he does not carry parasites or diseases that might be dangerous to your family.

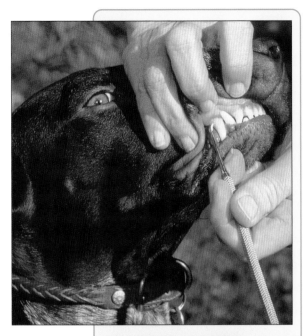

CARETAKER OF TEETH
You are your dog's caretaker and his dentist. Vets warn that plaque and tartar buildup on the teeth will damage the gums and allow bacteria to enter the dog's bloodstream, causing serious damage to the animal's vital organs. Studies show that over 50% of dogs have some form of gum disease before age three. Daily or weekly tooth cleaning (with a brush or soft gauze pad wipes) can add to your dog's life.

assistance as quickly as possible. As with all diseases, the earlier a problem is identified and treated, the more likely it is that the cure will be successful.

HEREDITARY SKIN DISORDERS
Veterinary dermatologists are currently researching a number of skin disorders that are believed to have hereditary basis. These inherited diseases are transmitted by both parents, who appear (phenotypically) normal but have a recessive gene for the disease, meaning that they carry, but are not affected by, the disease. These diseases pose serious problems to breeders because in some instances there are no methods of identifying carriers. Often the secondary diseases associated with these skin conditions are even more debilitating than the disorder itself, including cancers and respiratory problems.

Among the hereditary skin disorders for which the mode of inheritance is known, are acrodermatitis, cutaneous asthenia (Ehlers-Danlos syndrome), sebaceous adenitis, cyclic hematopoiesis, dermatomyositis, IgA deficiency, color dilution alopecia and nodular dermatofibrosis. Some of these disorders are limited to one or two breeds and others affect a large number of breeds. All inherited diseases must be diagnosed and treated by a veterinary specialist.

disorders. Pet shops sell many treatments for skin problems, but most of the treatments are directed at the symptoms and not the underlying problem(s). If your dog is suffering from a skin disorder, you should seek professional

"P" STANDS FOR PROBLEM

Urinary-tract disease is a serious condition that requires immediate medical attention. Symptoms include urinating in inappropriate places or the need to urinate frequently in small amounts. Urinary-tract disease is most effectively treated with antibiotics. To help promote good urinary-tract health, owners must always be sure that a constant supply of fresh water is available to their pets.

PARASITE BITES

Many of us are allergic to insect bites. The bites itch, erupt and may even become infected. Dogs have the same reaction to fleas, ticks and/or mites. When an insect lands on you, you have the chance to whisk it away with your hand. Unfortunately, when your dog is bitten by a flea, tick or mite, he can only scratch it away or bite it. By the time the dog has been bitten, the parasite has done some of its damage. It may also have laid eggs to cause further problems in the near future. The itching from parasite bites is probably due to the saliva injected into the site when the parasite sucks the dog's blood.

ACRAL LICK GRANULOMA

Many breeds have a very poorly understood syndrome called acral lick granuloma. The manifestation of the problem is the dog's tireless attack at a specific area of the body, almost always the legs or paws. The dog licks so intensively that he removes the hair and skin, leaving an ugly, large wound. Tiny protuberances, which are outgrowths of new capillaries, bead on the surface of the wound. Owners who notice their dogs' biting and chewing at their extremities should have the vet determine the cause. If lick granuloma is identified, although there is no absolute cure, corticosteroids are the most common treatment.

Your GSP needs fresh air and sunshine just like you do! After outdoor activities, check your dog's skin and coat to check for debris, insect bites or other irritants.

A SKUNKY PROBLEM

Have you noticed your dog dragging his rump along the floor? If so, it is likely that his anal sacs are impacted or possibly infected. The anal sacs are small pouches located on both sides of the anus under the skin and muscles. They are about the size and shape of a grape and contain a foul-smelling liquid. Their contents are usually emptied when the dog has a bowel movement but, if not emptied completely, they will impact, which will cause your dog much pain. Fortunately, your veterinarian can tend to this problem easily by draining the sacs for the dog. Be aware that your dog might also empty his anal sacs in cases of extreme fright.

AIRBORNE ALLERGIES

Just as humans have hay fever, rose fever and other fevers from which they suffer during the pollinating season, many dogs suffer from the same allergies. When the pollen count is high, your dog might suffer, but don't expect him to sneeze and have a runny nose like a human would.

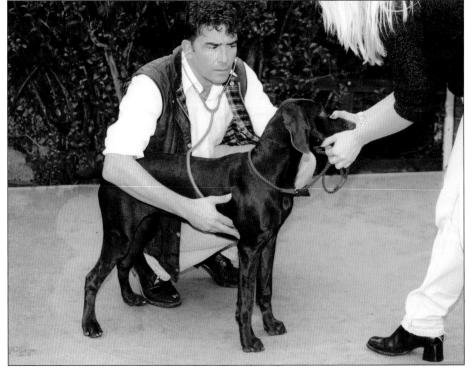

Regular veterinary exams are essential to your GSP's good health. Few vets these days make house calls, though large kennels will have a vet who visits.

Dogs react to pollen allergies the same way they react to fleas—they scratch and bite themselves.

Dogs, like humans, can be tested for allergens. Discuss the testing with your veterinary dermatologist.

AUTO-IMMUNE ILLNESSES
An auto-immune illness is one in which the immune system over-acts and does not recognize parts of the affected person; rather, the immune system starts to react as if these parts were foreign and need to be destroyed.

Lupus is an auto-immune disease that affects dogs as well as people. It can take variable forms, affecting the kidneys, bones and skin. It can be fatal, so is treated with steroids, which can them-selves have very significant side effects. The steroids calm down the allergic reaction to the body's tissues, which helps the lupus, but the steroids also decrease the body's reaction to real foreign substances such as bacteria, and also thin the skin and bones.

FOOD PROBLEMS

FOOD ALLERGIES
Dogs can be allergic to many foods that are best-sellers and highly recommended by breeders and veterinarians. Changing the brand of food that you buy may not eliminate the problem if the element to which the dog is

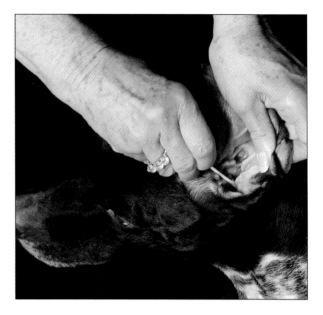

allergic is contained in the new brand.

Recognizing a food allergy is difficult. Humans vomit or have rashes when they eat a food to which they are allergic. Dogs neither vomit nor (usually) develop a rash. They react in the same manner as they do to an airborne or flea allergy: they itch, scratch and bite, thus making the diagnosis extremely difficult. While pollen allergies and para-site bites are usually seasonal, food allergies are year-round problems.

FOOD INTOLERANCE
Food intolerance is the inability of the dog to completely digest certain foods. For example, puppies that may have done very

Check and clean your GSP's ears regularly. It is much safer to use a cotton ball, though, as poking and prodding with a swab can be dangerous. *Never* enter the ear canal.

Administering
oral medication
to a dog can be a
challenge! One
method is to
place the pill in
the back of the
dog's mouth and
stroke his throat
to encourage him
to swallow.

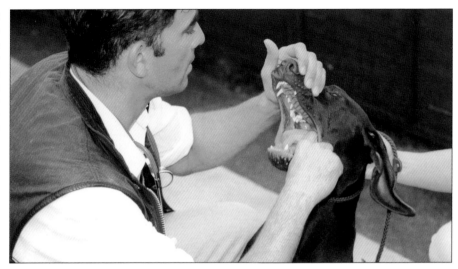

Administering oral medication to a dog can be a challenge! One method is to place the pill in the back of the dog's mouth and stroke his throat to encourage him to swallow.

well on their mother's milk may not do well on cow's milk. The result of food intolerance may be loose bowels, passing gas and stomach pains. These are the only obvious symptoms of food intolerance and that makes diagnosis difficult.

It is possible to handle food allergies and food intolerance yourself. Put your dog on a diet that he has never had. Obviously,

HOW TO PREVENT BLOAT

Research has confirmed that the structure of deep-chested breeds contributes to their predisposition to bloat. Nevertheless, there are several precautions that you can take to reduce the risk of this life-threatening condition:

• Feed your dog twice daily in smaller portions rather than offer one big meal.
• Do not exercise your dog for at least one hour before and two hours after he has eaten.
• Make certain that your dog is calm and not overly excited while he is eating. It has been proven that nervous or overly excited dogs are more prone to develop bloat.
• Add a small portion of moist meat product to his dry food ration.
• Serve his meals and water in an elevated bowl stand, which avoids the dog's craning his neck while eating and drinking.
• To prevent your dog from gobbling his food too quickly, and thereby swallowing air, put some large (unswallowable) toys into his bowl so that he will have to eat around them to get his food.
• Never allow your dog to gulp water.

DETECTING BLOAT

As important as it is to take precautions against bloat/gastric torsion, it is of equal important to recognize the symptoms. It is necessary for your German Shorthaired Pointer to get immediate veterinary attention if you notice any of the following signs:

• Your dog's stomach starts to distend, ending up large and as tight as a football;

• Your dog is dribbling, as no saliva can be swallowed;

• Your dog makes frequent attempts to vomit but cannot bring anything up due to the stomach's being closed off;

• Your dog is distressed from pain;

• Your dog starts to suffer from clinical shock, meaning that there is not enough blood in the dog's circulation as the hard, dilated stomach stops the blood from returning to the heart to be pumped around the body. Clinical shock is indicated by pale gums and tongue, as they have been starved of blood. The shocked dog also has glazed, staring eyes.

You have minutes, yes *minutes*, to get your dog into surgery. If you see any of these symptoms at any time of the day or night, get to the vet immediately. Someone will have to phone and warn that you are on your way (which is a justification for the invention of the cellular phone!), so that they can be prepared to get your pet on the operating table.

if he has never eaten this new food, he can't yet have been allergic or intolerant of it. Start with a single ingredient that is not in the dog's diet at the present time. Ingredients like chopped beef or chicken are common in dogs' diets, so try another protein source like fish, rabbit or even something exotic like pheasant. Keep the dog on this diet (with no additives) for a month. If the symptoms of food allergy or intolerance disappear, chances are your dog has a food allergy.

Don't think that the single ingredient cured the problem. You still must find a suitable diet and ascertain which ingredi-ent in the old diet was objectionable. This is most easily done by adding ingredients to the new diet one at a time. Let the dog stay on the modified diet for a month before you add another ingredient. Eventually, you will determine the ingredient that caused the adverse reaction.

An alternative method is to carefully study the ingredients in the diet to which your dog is allergic or intolerant. Identify the main ingredient in this diet and eliminate the main ingredient by buying a different food that does not have that ingredient. Keep experimenting until the symptoms disappear after one month on the new diet.

A male dog flea, *Ctenocephalides canis.*

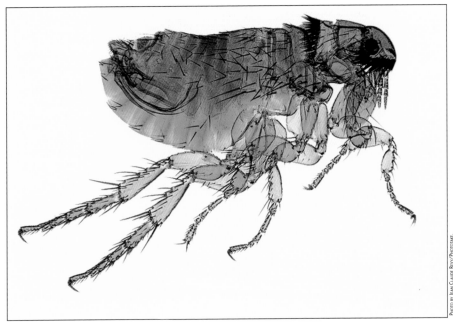

PHOTO BY JEAN CLAUDE REVY/PHOTOTAKE.

EXTERNAL PARASITES

FLEAS

Of all the problems to which dogs are prone, none is more well known and frustrating than fleas. Flea infestation is relatively simple to cure but difficult to prevent. Parasites that are harbored inside the body are a bit more difficult to eradicate but they are easier to control.

To control flea infestation, you have to understand the flea's life cycle. Fleas are often thought of as a summertime problem, but centrally heated homes have changed the patterns and fleas can be found at any time of the year. The most effective method of flea control is a two-stage approach: one stage to kill the adult fleas, and the other to control the development of pre-adult fleas. Unfortunately, no single active ingredient is effective against all stages of the life cycle.

FLEA KILLER CAUTION— "POISON"

Flea-killers are poisonous. You should not spray these toxic chemicals on areas of a dog's body that he licks, including his genitals and his face. Flea killers taken internally are a better answer, but check with your vet in case internal therapy is not advised for your dog.

LIFE CYCLE STAGES

During its life, a flea will pass through four life stages: egg, larva, pupa or nymph and adult. The adult stage is the most visible and irritating stage of the flea life cycle, and this is why the majority of flea-control products concentrate on this stage. The fact is that adult fleas account for only 1% of the total flea population, and the other 99% exist in pre-adult stages, i.e., eggs, larvae and nymphs. The pre-adult stages are barely visible to the naked eye.

THE LIFE CYCLE OF THE FLEA

Eggs are laid on the dog, usually in quantities of about 20 or 30, several times a day. The adult female flea must have a blood meal before each egg-laying session. When first laid, the eggs will cling to the dog's hair, as the eggs are still moist. However, they will quickly dry out and fall from the dog, especially if the dog moves around or scratches. Many eggs will fall off in the dog's favorite area or an area in which he spends a lot of time, such as his bed.

Once the eggs fall from the dog onto the carpet or furniture, they will hatch into larvae. This takes from one to ten days. Larvae are not particularly mobile and will usually travel only a few inches from where they hatch. However, they do have a tendency to move away from bright light and heavy

> ### EN GARDE:
> ### CATCHING FLEAS OFF GUARD!
> Consider the following ways to arm yourself against fleas:
> - Add a small amount of pennyroyal or eucalyptus oil to your dog's bath. These natural remedies repel fleas.
> - Supplement your dog's food with fresh garlic (minced or grated) and an hearty amount of brewer's yeast, both of which ward off fleas.
> - Use a flea comb on your dog daily. Submerge fleas in a cup of bleach to kill them quickly.
> - Confine the dog to only a few rooms to limit the spread of fleas in the home.
> - Vacuum daily...and get all of the crevices! Dispose of the bag every few days until the problem is under control.
> - Wash your dog's bedding daily. Cover cushions where your dog sleeps with towels, and wash the towels often.

traffic—under furniture and behind doors are common places to find high quantities of flea larvae.

The flea larvae feed on dead organic matter, including adult flea feces, until they are ready to change into adult fleas. Fleas will usually remain as larvae for around seven days. After this period, the larvae will pupate into protective pupae. While inside the pupae, the larvae will undergo

Fleas have been measured as being able to jump 300,000 times and can jump 150 times their length in any direction, including straight up.

metamorphosis and change into adult fleas. This can take as little time as a few days, but the adult fleas can remain inside the pupae waiting to hatch for up to two years. The pupae are signaled to hatch by certain stimuli, such as physical pressure—the pupae's being stepped on, heat from an animal's lying on the pupae or increased carbon-dioxide levels and vibrations—indicating that a suitable host is available.

Once hatched, the adult flea must feed within a few days. Once the adult flea finds a host, it will not leave voluntarily. It only becomes dislodged by grooming or the host animal's scratching.

PHOTO BY DWIGHT R. KUHN

The adult flea will remain on the host for the duration of its life unless forcibly removed.

TREATING THE ENVIRONMENT AND THE DOG

Treating fleas should be a two-pronged attack. First, the environment needs to be treated; this includes carpets and furniture, especially the dog's bedding and areas underneath furniture. The environment should be treated with a household spray containing an Insect Growth Regulator (IGR) and an insecticide to kill the adult fleas. Most IGRs are effective against eggs and larvae; they actually mimic the fleas' own hormones and stop the eggs and larvae from developing into adult fleas. There are currently no treatments available to attack the pupa stage of the life cycle, so the adult insecticide is used to kill the newly hatched adult fleas before they find a host. Most IGRs are active for many months, while

A scanning electron micrograph of a dog or cat flea, *Ctenocephalides*, magnified more than 100x. This image has been colorized for effect.

S. E. M. BY DR. DENNIS KUNKEL, UNIVERSITY OF HAWAII

THE LIFE CYCLE OF THE FLEA

Adult

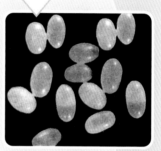

Egg

Larva

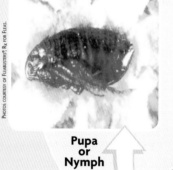

**Pupa
or
Nymph**

A LOOK AT FLEAS

Fleas have been around for millions of years and have adapted to changing host animals. They are able to go through a complete life cycle in less than one month or they can extend their lives to almost two years by remaining as pupae or cocoons. They do not need blood or any other food for up to 20 months.

INSECT GROWTH REGULATOR (IGR)

Two types of products should be used when treating fleas—a product to treat the pet and a product to treat the home. Adult fleas represent less than 1% of the flea population. The pre-adult fleas (eggs, larvae and pupae) represent more than 99% of the flea population and are found in the environment; it is in the case of pre-adult fleas that products containing an Insect Growth Regulator (IGR) should be used in the home.

IGRs are a new class of compounds used to prevent the development of insects. They do not kill the insect outright, but instead use the insect's biology against it to stop it from completing its growth. Products that contain methoprene are the world's first and leading IGRs. Used to control fleas and other insects, this type of IGR will stop flea larvae from developing and protect the house for up to seven months.

The American dog tick, *Dermacentor variabilis*, is probably the most common tick found on dogs. Look at the strength in its eight legs! No wonder it's hard to detach them.

adult insecticides are only active for a few days.

When treating with a household spray, it is a good idea to vacuum before applying the product. This stimulates as many pupae as possible to hatch into adult fleas. The vacuum cleaner should also be treated with an insecticide to prevent the eggs and larvae that have been collected in the vacuum bag from hatching.

The second stage of treatment is to apply an adult insecticide to the dog. Traditionally, this would be in the form of a collar or a spray, but more recent innovations include digestible insecticides that poison the fleas when they ingest the dog's blood. Alternatively, there are drops that, when placed on the back of the dog's neck, spread throughout the hair and skin to kill adult fleas.

TICKS

Though not as common as fleas, ticks are found all over the tropical and temperate world. They don't bite, like fleas; they harpoon. They dig their sharp proboscis (nose) into the dog's skin and drink the blood. Their

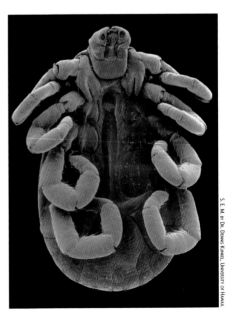

S. E. M. BY DR. DENNIS KUNKEL, UNIVERSITY OF HAWAII

only food and drink is dog's blood. Dogs can get Lyme disease, Rocky Mountain spotted fever, tick bite paralysis and many other diseases from ticks. They may live where fleas are found and they like to hide in cracks or seams in walls. They are controlled the same way fleas are controlled.

The American dog tick, *Dermacentor variabilis*, may well be the most common dog tick in many geographical areas, especially those areas where the climate is hot and humid. Most dog ticks have life expectancies of a week to six months, depending upon climatic conditions. They can neither jump nor fly, but they can crawl slowly and can range up to 16 feet to reach a sleeping or unsuspecting dog.

MITES

Just as fleas and ticks can be problematic for your dog, mites can also lead to an itchy nuisance. Microscopic in size, mites are related to ticks and generally take up permanent residence on their host animal—in this case, your dog! The term *mange* refers to any infestation caused by one of the mighty mites, of which there are six varieties that concern dog owners.

Demodex mites cause a condition known as demodicosis

DEER-TICK CROSSING
The great outdoors may be fun for your dog, but it also is an home to dangerous ticks. Deer ticks carry a bacterium known as *Borrelia burgdorferi* and are most active in the autumn and spring. When infections are caught early, penicillin and tetracycline are effective antibiotics, but if left untreated the bacteria may cause neurological, kidney and cardiac problems as well as long-term trouble with walking and painful joints.

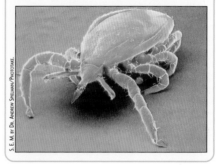

S. E. M. BY DR. ANDREW SPIELMAN/PHOTOTAKE.

PHOTO BY DR. DENNIS KUNKEL, UNIVERSITY OF HAWAII.

The head of an American dog tick, *Dermacentor variabilis*, enlarged and colorized for effect.

The mange mite, *Psoroptes bovis*, can infest cattle and other domestic animals.

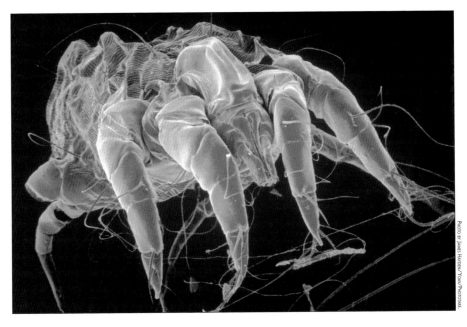

Photo by James Hayden/Yoav/Phototake.

(sometimes called red mange or follicular mange), in which the mites live in the dog's hair follicles and sebaceous glands. This type of mange is commonly passed from the dam to her puppies and usually shows up on the puppies' muzzles, though demodicosis is not transferable from one normal dog to another. Most dogs recover from this type of mange without any treatment, though topical therapies are commonly prescribed by the vet.

The *Cheyletiellosis* mite is the hook-mouthed culprit associated with "walking dandruff," a condition that affects dogs as well as cats and rabbits. This mite lives on the surface of the animal's skin and is readily transferable through direct or indirect contact with an affected animal. The dandruff is present in the form of scaly skin, which may or may not be itchy. If not treated, this mange can affect a whole kennel of dogs and can be spread to humans as well.

The *Sarcoptes* mite causes intense itching on the dog in the form of a condition known as scabies or sarcoptic mange. The cycle of the *Sarcoptes* mite lasts about three weeks, and the mites live in the top layer of the dog's

Human lice look like dog lice; the two are closely related.

Photo by Dwight R. Kuhn.

skin (epidermis), preferably in areas with little hair. Scabies is highly contagious and can be passed to humans. Sometimes an allergic reaction to the mite worsens the severe itching associated with sarcoptic mange.

Ear mites, *Otodectes cynotis*, lead to otodectic mange, which most commonly affects the outer ear canal of the dog, though other areas can be affected as well. Dogs with ear-mite infestation commonly scratch at their ears, causing further irritation, and shake their heads. Dark brown droppings in the outer ear confirm the diagnosis. Your vet can prescribe a treatment to flush out the ears and kill any eggs in the ears. A complete month of treatment is necessary to cure the mange.

Two other mites, less common in dogs, include *Dermanyssus gallinae* (the poultry or red mite) and *Eutrombicula alfreddugesi* (the North American mite associated with trombiculidiasis or chigger infestation). The poultry mite frequently lives on chickens, but can transfer to dogs who spend time near farm animals. Chigger

DO NOT MIX
Never mix pest control products without first consulting your vet. Some products can become toxic when combined with others and can cause fatal consequences.

NOT A DROP TO DRINK
Never allow your dog to swim in polluted water or public areas where water quality can be suspect. Even perfectly clear water can harbour parasites, many of which can cause serious to fatal illnesses in canines. Areas inhabited by water-fowl and other wildlife are especially dangerous.

infestation affects dogs in the Central US who have exposure to woodlands. The types of mange caused by both of these mites are treatable by veterinarians.

INTERNAL PARASITES
Most animals—fishes, birds and mammals, including dogs and humans—have worms and other parasites that live inside their bodies. According to Dr. Herbert R. Axelrod, the fish pathologist, there are two kinds of parasites: dumb and smart. The smart parasites live in peaceful cooperation with their hosts (symbiosis), while the dumb parasites kill their hosts. Most worm infections are relatively easy to control. If they are not controlled, they weaken the host dog to the point that other medical problems occur, but they do not kill the host as dumb parasites would.

A brown dog tick, *Rhipicephalus sanguineus*, is an uncommon but annoying tick found on dogs.
PHOTO BY CAROLINA BIOLOGICAL SUPPLY/PHOTOTAKE.

Photo by Carolina Biological Supply/Phototake.

The roundworm *Rhabditis* can infect both dogs and humans.

ROUNDWORMS

Average-size dogs can pass 1,360,000 roundworm eggs every day. For example, if there were only 1 million dogs in the world, the world would be saturated with thousands of tons of dog feces. These feces would contain around 15,000,000,000 roundworm eggs.

Up to 31% of home yards and children's sand boxes in the US contain roundworm eggs.

Flushing dog's feces down the toilet is not a safe practice because the usual sewage treatments do not destroy roundworm eggs.

Infected puppies start shedding roundworm eggs at three weeks of age. They can be infected by their mother's milk.

The roundworm, *Ascaris lumbricoides.*

Photo by Dwight R. Kuhn.

ROUNDWORMS

The roundworms that infect dogs are known scientifically as *Toxocara canis.* They live in the dog's intestines and shed eggs continually. It has been estimated that a dog produces about 6 or more ounces of feces every day. Each ounce of feces averages hundreds of thousands of roundworm eggs. There are no known areas in which dogs roam that do not contain roundworm eggs. The greatest danger of roundworms is that they infect people, too! It is wise to have your dog tested regularly for roundworms.

In young puppies, roundworms cause bloated bellies, diarrhea, coughing and vomiting, and are transmitted from the dam (through blood or milk). Affected puppies will not appear as animated as normal puppies. The worms appear spaghetti-like, measuring as long as 6 inches. Adult dogs can acquire roundworms through coprophagia (eating contaminated feces) or by killing rodents that carry roundworms.

Roundworm infection can kill puppies and cause severe problems in adults, as the hatched larvae travel to the lungs and trachea through the bloodstream. Cleanliness is the best preventative for roundworms. Always pick up after your dog and dispose of feces in appropriate receptacles.

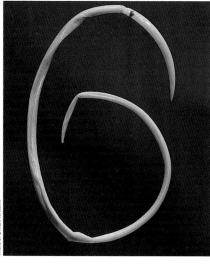

PHOTO BY DWIGHT R. KUHN.

HOOKWORMS

In the United States, dog owners have to be concerned about four different species of hookworm, the most common and most serious of which is *Ancylostoma caninum,* which prefers warm climates. The others are *Ancylostoma braziliense, Ancylostoma tubaeforme* and *Uncinaria stenocephala,* the latter of which is a concern to dogs living in the Northern US and Canada, as this species prefers cold climates. Hookworms are dangerous to humans as well as to dogs and cats, and can be the cause of severe anemia due to iron deficiency. The worm uses its teeth to attach itself to the dog's intestines and changes the site of its attachment about six times per day. Each time the worm repositions itself, the dog loses

blood and can become anemic. *Ancylostoma caninum* is the most likely of the four species to cause anemia in the dog.

Symptoms of hookworm infection include dark stools, weight loss, general weakness, pale coloration and anemia, as well as possible skin problems. Fortunately, hookworms are easily purged from the affected dog with a number of medications that have proven effective. Discuss these with your veterinarian. Most heartworm preventatives include a hookworm insecticide as well.

Owners also must be aware that hookworms can infect humans, who can acquire the larvae through exposure to contaminated feces. Since the worms cannot complete their life cycle on a human, the worms simply infest the skin and cause irritation. This condition is known as cutaneous larva migrans syndrome. As a preventative, use disposable gloves or a "poop-scoop" to pick up your dog's droppings and prevent your dog (or neighborhood cats) from defecating in children's play areas.

The hookworm *Ancylostoma caninum.*

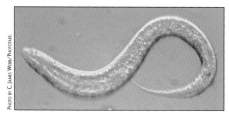

PHOTO BY C. JAMES WEBB/PHOTOTAKE.

The infective stage of the hookworm larva.

TAPEWORMS

Humans, rats, squirrels, foxes, coyotes, wolves and domestic dogs are all susceptible to tapeworm infection. Except in humans, tapeworms are usually not a fatal infection. Infected individuals can harbor 1000 parasitic worms.

Tapeworms, like some other types of worm, are hermaphroditic, meaning male and female in the same worm.

If dogs eat infected rats or mice, or anything else injected with tapeworm, they get the tapeworm disease. One month after attaching to a dog's intestine, the worm starts shedding eggs. These eggs are infective immediately. Infective eggs can live for a few months without a host animal.

The head and rostellum (the round prominence on the scolex) of a tapeworm, which infects dogs and humans.

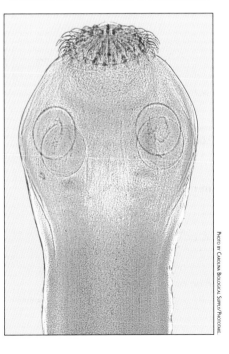

PHOTO BY CAROLINA BIOLOGICAL SUPPLY/PHOTOTAKE.

TAPEWORMS

There are many species of tapeworm, all of which are carried by fleas! The most common tapeworm affecting dogs is known as *Dipylidium caninum*. The dog eats the flea and starts the tapeworm cycle. Humans can also be infected with tapeworms—so don't eat fleas! Fleas are so small that your dog could pass them onto your hands, your plate or your food and thus make it possible for you to ingest a flea that is carrying tapeworm eggs.

While tapeworm infection is not life-threatening in dogs (smart parasite!), it can be the cause of a very serious liver disease for humans. About 50% of the humans infected with *Echinococcus multilocularis*, a type of tapeworm that causes alveolar hydatid, perish.

WHIPWORMS

In North America, whipworms are counted among the most common parasitic worms in dogs. The whipworm's scientific name is *Trichuris vulpis*. These worms attach themselves in the lower parts of the intestine, where they feed. Affected dogs may only experience upset tummies, colic and diarrhea. These worms, however, can live for months or years in the dog, beginning their larval stage in the small intestine, spending their adult stage in the large intestine and finally passing infective eggs through the dog's feces. The only way to detect whipworms is through a fecal examination, though this is not always foolproof. Treatment for whipworms is tricky, due to the worms' unusual life-cycle pattern, and very often dogs are reinfected due to exposure to infective eggs on the ground. The whipworm eggs can survive in the environment for as long as five years, thus cleaning up droppings in your own backyard as well as in public places is absolutely essential for sanitation purposes and the health of your dog.

THREADWORMS

Though less common than round-worms, hookworms and those listed above, threadworms concern dog owners in the Southwestern US and Gulf Coast area where the climate is hot and humid. Living in the small intestine of the dog, this worm measures a mere 2 millimeters and is round in shape. Like that of the whipworm, the threadworm's life cycle is very complex and the eggs and larvae are passed through the feces. A deadly disease in humans, *Strongyloides* readily infects people, and the handling of feces is the most common means of transmission. Threadworms are most often seen in young puppies; bloody diarrhea and pneumonia are symptoms. Sick puppies must be isolated and treated immediately; vets recommend a follow-up treatment one month later.

HEARTWORM PREVENTATIVES

There are many heartworm preventatives on the market, many of which are sold at your veterinarian's office. These products can be given daily or monthly, depending on the manufacturer's instructions. All of these preventatives contain chemical insecticides directed at killing heartworms, which leads to some controversy among dog owners. In effect, heartworm preventatives are necessary evils, though you should determine how necessary based on your pet's lifestyle. There is no doubt that heartworm is a dreadful disease that threatens the life of dogs. However, the likelihood of your dog's being bitten by an infected mosquito is slim in most places, and a mosquito-repellent (or an herbal remedy such as Wormwood or Black Walnut) is much safer for your dog and will not compromise his immune system (the way heartworm preventatives will). Should you decide to use the traditional preventative "medications," you can consider giving the pill every other or third month. Since the toxins in the pill will kill the heartworms at all stages of development, the pill would be effective in killing larvae, nymphs or adults and it takes four months for the larvae to reach the adult stage. Thus, there is no rationale to poisoning the dog's system on a monthly basis. Lastly, do not give the pill during the winter months since there are no mosquitoes around to pass on their infection, unless you live in a tropical environment.

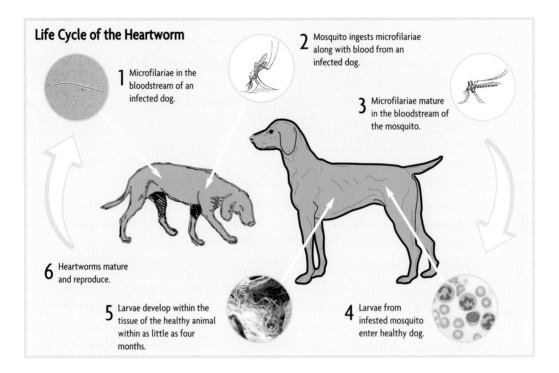

Life Cycle of the Heartworm

1 Microfilariae in the bloodstream of an infected dog.

2 Mosquito ingests microfilariae along with blood from an infected dog.

3 Microfilariae mature in the bloodstream of the mosquito.

4 Larvae from infested mosquito enter healthy dog.

5 Larvae develop within the tissue of the healthy animal within as little as four months.

6 Heartworms mature and reproduce.

HEARTWORMS

Heartworms are thin, extended worms up to 12 inches long, which live in a dog's heart and the major blood vessels surrounding it. Dogs may have up to 200 worms. Symptoms may be loss of energy, loss of appetite, coughing, the development of a pot belly and anemia.

Heartworms are transmitted by mosquitoes. The mosquito drinks the blood of an infected dog and takes in larvae with the blood. The larvae, called microfilariae, develop within the body of the mosquito and are passed on to the next dog bitten after the larvae

mature. It takes two to three weeks for the larvae to develop to the infective stage within the body of the mosquito. Dogs are usually treated at about six weeks of age and maintained on a prophylactic dose given monthly.

Blood testing for heartworms is not necessarily indicative of how seriously your dog is infected. Although this is a dangerous disease, it is not easy for a dog to be infected. Discuss the various preventatives with your vet, as there are many different types now available. Together you can decide on a safe course of prevention for your dog.

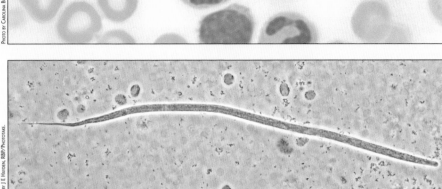

Magnified heart-
worm larvae, *Diro-
filaria immitis.*

Heartworm, *Diro-
filaria immitis.*

The heart
of a dog infected
with canine heart-
worm, *Dirofilaria
immitis.*

HOMEOPATHY:

an alternative
to conventional
medicine

"Less is Most"

Using this principle, the strength of a homeopathic remedy is measured by the number of serial dilutions that were undertaken to create it. The greater the number of serial dilutions, the greater the strength of the homeopathic remedy. The potency of a remedy that has been made by making a dilution of 1 part in 100 parts (or 1/100) is 1c or 1cH. If this remedy is subjected to a series of further dilutions, each one being 1/100, a more dilute and stronger remedy is produced. If the remedy is diluted in this way six times, it is called 6c or 6cH. A dilution of 6c is 1 part in 1,000,000,000,000. In general, higher potencies in more frequent doses are better for acute symptoms and lower potencies in more infrequent doses are more useful for chronic, long-standing problems.

CURING OUR DOGS NATURALLY

Holistic medicine means treating the whole animal as a unique, perfect living being. Generally, holistic treatments do not suppress the symptoms that the body naturally produces, as do most medications prescribed by conventional doctors and vets. Holistic methods seek to cure disease by regaining balance and harmony in the patient's environment. Some of these methods include use of nutritional therapy, herbs, flower essences, aromatherapy, acupuncture, massage, chiropractic and, of course the most popular holistic approach, homeopathy.

Homeopathy is a theory or system of treating illness with small doses of substances which, if administered in larger quantities, would produce the symptoms that the patient already has. This approach is often described as "like cures like." Although modern veterinary medicine is geared toward the "quick fix," homeopathy relies on the belief that, given the time, the body is able to heal itself and return to its natural, healthy state.

Choosing a remedy to cure a problem in our dogs is the difficult part of homeopathy. Consult with your veterinarian for a professional diagnosis of your dog's symptoms.

Often these symptoms require immediate conventional care. If your vet is willing and knowledgeable, you may attempt a homeopathic remedy. Be aware that cortisone prevents homeopathic remedies from working. There are hundreds of possibilities and combinations to cure many problems in dogs, from basic physical problems such as excessive shedding, fleas or other parasites, unattractive doggy odor, bad breath, obesity, upset tummy, dry, oily or dull coat, diarrhea, ear problems or eye discharge (including tears and dry or mucousy matter), to behavioral abnormalities such as fear of loud noises, habitual licking, poor appetite, excessive barking and various phobias. From alumina to zincum metallicum, the remedies span the planet and the imagination…from flowers and weeds to chemicals, insect droppings, diesel smoke and volcanic ash.

Using "Like to Treat Like"

Unlike conventional medicines that suppress symptoms, homeopathic remedies treat illnesses with small doses of substances that, if administered in larger quantities, would produce the symptoms that the patient already has. While the same homeopathic remedy can be used to treat different symptoms in different dogs, here are some interesting remedies and their uses.

Apis Mellifica
(made from honey bee venom) can be used for allergies or to reduce swelling that occurs in acutely infected kidneys.

Diesel Smoke
can be used to help control travel sickness.

Calcarea Fluorica
(made from calcium fluoride, which helps harden bone structure) can be useful in treating hard lumps in tissues.

Natrum Muriaticum
(made from common salt, sodium chloride) is useful in treating thin, thirsty dogs.

Nitricum Acidum
(made from nitric acid) is used for symptoms you would expect to see from contact with acids such as lesions, especially where the skin joins the linings of body orifices or openings such as the lips and nostrils.

Symphytum
(made from the herb Knitbone, *Symphytum officianale*) is used to encourage bones to heal.

Urtica Urens
(made from the common stinging nettle) is used in treating painful, irritating rashes.

First Aid at a Glance

Burns
Place the affected area under cool water; use ice if only a small area is burnt.

Bee Stings/Insect bites
Apply ice to relieve swelling; antihistamine dosed properly.

Animal bites
Clean any bleeding area; apply pressure until bleeding subsides; go to the vet.

Spider bites
Use cold compress and a pressurized pack to inhibit venom's spreading.

Antifreeze poisoning
Induce vomiting with hydrogen peroxide. Seek *immediate* veterinary help!

Fish hooks
Removal best handled by vet; hook must be cut in order to remove.

Snake bites
Pack ice around bite; contact vet quickly; identify snake for proper antivenin.

Car accident
Move dog from roadway with blanket; seek veterinary aid.

Shock
Calm the dog, keep him warm; seek immediate veterinary help.

Nosebleed
Apply cold compress to the nose; apply pressure to any visible abrasion.

Bleeding
Apply pressure above the area; treat wound by applying a cotton pack.

Heat stroke
Submerge dog in cold bath; cool down with fresh air and water; go to the vet.

Frostbite/Hypothermia
Warm the dog with a warm bath, electric blankets or hot water bottles.

Abrasions
Clean the wound and wash out thoroughly with fresh water; apply antiseptic.

Remember: an injured dog may attempt to bite a helping hand from fear and confusion. Always muzzle the dog before trying to offer assistance.

Recognizing a Sick Dog

Unlike colicky babies and cranky children, our canine kids cannot tell us when they are feeling ill. Therefore, there are a number of signs that owners can identify to know that their dogs are not feeling well.

Take note for physical manifestations such as:

- unusual, bad odor, including bad breath
- excessive shedding
- wax in the ears, chronic ear irritation
- oily, flaky, dull haircoat
- mucus, tearing or similar discharge in the eyes
- fleas or mites
- mucus in stool, diarrhea
- sensitivity to petting or handling
- licking at paws, scratching face, etc.

Keep an eye out for behavioral changes as well including:

- lethargy, idleness
- lack of patience or general irritability
- lack of appetite
- phobias (fear of people, loud noises, etc.)
- strange behavior, suspicion, fear
- coprophagia
- more frequent barking
- whimpering, crying

Get Well Soon

You don't need a DVM to provide good TLC to your sick or recovering dog, but you do need to pay attention to some details that normally wouldn't bother him. The following tips will aid Fido's recovery and get him back on his paws again:

- Keep his space free of irritating smells, like heavy perfumes and air fresheners.
- Rest is the best medicine! Avoid harsh lighting that will prevent your dog from sleeping. Shade him from bright sunlight during the day and dim the lights in the evening.
- Keep the noise level down. Animals are more sensitive to sound when they are sick.

- Be attentive to any necessary temperature adjustments. A dog with a fever needs a cool room and cold liquids. A bitch that is whelping or recovering from surgery will be more comfortable in a warm room, consuming warm liquids and food.
- You wouldn't send a sick child back to school early, so don't rush your dog back into a full routine until he seems absolutely ready.

CDS: COGNITIVE DYSFUNCTION SYNDROME
"OLD-DOG SYNDROME"

There are many ways for you to evaluate old-dog syndrome. Veterinarians have defined CDS (cognitive dysfunction syndrome) as the gradual deterioration of cognitive abilities. These are indicated by changes in the dog's behavior. When a dog changes his routine response, and maladies have been eliminated as the cause of these behavioral changes, then CDS is the usual diagnosis.

More than half the dogs over eight years old suffer from some form of CDS. The older the dog, the more chance he has of suffering from CDS. In humans, doctors often dismiss the CDS behavioral changes as part of "winding down."

There are four major signs of CDS: frequent potty accidents inside the home, sleeping much more or much less than normal, acting confused and failing to respond to social stimuli.

SYMPTOMS OF CDS

FREQUENT POTTY ACCIDENTS
- *Urinates in the house.*
- *Defecates in the house.*
- *Doesn't signal that he wants to go out.*

SLEEP PATTERNS
- *Moves much more slowly.*
- *Sleeps more than normal during the day.*
- *Sleeps less during the night.*

CONFUSION
- *Goes outside and just stands there.*
- *Appears confused with a faraway look in his eyes.*
- *Hides more often.*
- *Doesn't recognize friends.*
- *Doesn't come when called.*
- *Walks around listlessly and without a destination goal.*

FAILURE TO RESPOND TO SOCIAL STIMULI
- *Comes to people less frequently, whether called or not.*
- *Doesn't tolerate petting for more than a short time.*
- *Doesn't come to the door when you return home from work.*

GERMAN SHORTHAIRED POINTER

The term *old* is a qualitative term. For dogs, as well as their masters, old is relative. Certainly we can all distinguish between a puppy German Shorthaired Pointer and an adult German Shorthaired Pointer—there are the obvious physical traits, such as size, appearance and facial expressions, as well as personality traits. Puppies and young dogs like to play with children. Children's natural exuberance is a good match for the seemingly endless energy of young dogs. They like to run, jump, chase and retrieve. When dogs grow older and cease their interaction with children, they are often thought of as being too old to play with the kids. On the other hand, if a German Shorthaired Pointer is only exposed to people with quieter lifestyles, his life will usually be less active and the decrease in energy level as he ages will not be as obvious.

If people live to be 100 years old, dogs live to be 20 years old. While this is a good rule of thumb, it is very inaccurate. When trying to compare dog years to human years, you cannot make a generalization about all dogs. You can make the generalization that 14 years is a good lifespan for a German Shorthaired Pointer, which is quite good compared to many other pure-bred dogs that may only live to 8 or 9 years of age. Some German Shorthaired Pointers have been known to live to 16 years. Dogs are generally considered mature within three years, but they can reproduce even earlier. So, again to generalize, the first three years of a dog's life are like seven times that of comparable humans. That means a 3-year-old dog is like a 21-year-

HORMONAL PROBLEMS
Although graying is normal and expected in older dogs, a flaky coat or loss of hair is not. Such coat problems may point to a hormonal problem. Hypothyroidism, in which the thyroid gland fails to produce the normal amount of hormones, is one such problem. Your vet can treat hypothyroidism with an oral supplement. The condition is more common in certain breeds, so discuss its likelihood in your dog with your breeder and vet.

old human. However, there is no hard and fast rule for comparing dog and human ages. The comparison is made even more difficult, for not all dogs and not all humans age at the same rate...and human females live longer than human males.

WHAT TO LOOK FOR IN SENIORS

Most veterinarians and behaviorists use the seven-year mark as the time to consider a dog a senior. The term *senior* does not imply that the dog is geriatric and has begun to fail in mind and body. Aging is essentially a slowing process. Humans readily admit that they feel a difference in their activity level from age 20 to 30, and then from 30 to 40, etc. By treating the seven-year-old dog as a senior, owners are able to implement certain therapeutic and preventative medical strategies with the help of their vets.

A senior-care program should include at least two veterinary visits per year and screening sessions to determine the dog's health status, as well as nutritional counseling. Veterinarians determine the senior dog's health status through a blood smear for a complete blood count, serum chemistry profile with electrolytes, urinalysis, blood pressure

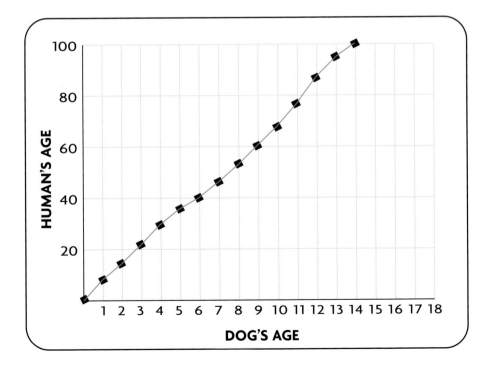

check, electrocardiogram, ocular tonometry (pressure on the eyeball) and dental prophylaxis.

Such an extensive program for senior dogs is well advised before owners start to see the obvious physical signs of aging, such as slower and inhibited movement, graying, increased sleep/nap periods and disinterest in play and other activity. This preventative program promises a longer, healthier life for the aging dog. Among the physical problems common in aging dogs are the loss of sight and hearing, arthritis, kidney and liver failure, diabetes mellitus, heart disease and Cushing's disease (a hormonal disease).

In addition to the physical manifestations discussed, there are some behavioral changes and problems related to aging dogs. Dogs suffering from hearing or vision loss, dental discomfort or arthritis can become aggressive. Likewise, the near-deaf and/or blind dog may be startled more easily and react in an unexpectedly aggressive manner. Seniors suffering from senility can become more impatient and irritable. Housesoiling accidents are associated with loss of mobility, kidney problems, loss of sphincter control as well as plaque accumulation, physiological brain changes and reactions to medications. Older dogs, just like young puppies, suffer from separation anxiety, which can lead to exces-

AN ANCIENT ACHE

As ancient a disease as any, arthritis remains poorly explained for human and dog alike. Fossils dating back 100 million years show the deterioration caused by arthritis. Human fossils two million years old show the disease in man. The most common type of arthritis affecting dogs is known as osteoarthritis, which occurs in adult dogs before their senior years. Obesity aggravating the dog's joints has been cited as a factor in arthritis.

Rheumatoid disease destroys joint cartilage and causes arthritic joints. Pituitary dysfunctions as well as diabetes have been associated with arthritis. Veterinarians treat arthritis variously, including aspirin, "bed rest" in the dog's crate, physical therapy and exercise, heat therapy (with a heating pad), providing soft bedding materials and treatment with corticosteroids (to reduce pain and swelling temporarily). Your vet will be able to recommend a course of action to help relieve your arthritic pal.

sive barking, whining, housesoiling and destructive behavior. Seniors may become fearful of everyday sounds, such as vacuum cleaners, heaters, thunder and passing traffic. Some dogs have difficulty sleeping, due to discomfort, the need for frequent potty visits and the like.

Owners should avoid spoiling the older dog with too many fatty treats. Obesity is a common problem in older dogs and subtracts years from their lives. Keep the senior dog as trim as possible since excessive weight puts additional stress on the body's vital organs. Some breeders recommend supplementing the diet with foods high in fiber and lower in calories. Adding fresh vegetables and marrow broth to the senior's diet makes a tasty, low-calorie, low-fat supplement. Vets also offer specialty diets or may recommend supplements for senior dogs that are worth exploring.

Your dog, as he nears his twilight years, needs his owner's patience and good care more than ever. Never punish an older dog

KEEP IT CONSISTENT

Puppies and older dogs are very similar in their need for consistency in their lives. Older pets may experience hearing and vision loss, or may just be more easily confused by changes in their homes. Try to keep things consistent for the senior dog. For example, doors that are always open or closed should remain so. Most importantly, don't dismiss a pet just because he's getting old; most senior dogs remain active and important parts of their owners' lives.

for an accident or abnormal behavior. For all the years of love, protection and companionship that your dog has provided, he

In ticked dogs, graying around the muzzle will not be so obvious. Gray hairs around the eyes and increased rest periods will be more noticeable signs of aging.

deserves special attention and courtesies. The older dog may need to relieve himself at 3 a.m. because he can no longer hold it for eight hours. Older dogs may not be able to remain crated for more than two or three hours. It may be time to give up a sofa or chair to your old friend. Although he may not seem as enthusiastic about your attention and petting, he does appreciate the considerations you offer as he gets older.

Your German Shorthaired Pointer does not understand why his world is slowing down. Owners must make the transition into the golden years as pleasant and rewarding as possible.

WHAT TO DO WHEN THE TIME COMES

You are never fully prepared to make a rational decision about putting your dog to sleep. It is very obvious that you love your German Shorthaired Pointer or you would not be reading this book. Putting a loved dog to sleep is extremely difficult. It is a decision that must be made with your veterinarian. You are usually forced to make the decision when one of the life-threatening symptoms listed above becomes serious enough for you to seek medical (veterinary) help.

If the prognosis of the malady indicates the end is near and your beloved pet will only suffer more and experience no enjoyment for

> **KEEPING SENIORS WARM**
> The coats of many older dogs become thinner as they age, which makes them more sensitive to cold temperatures and more susceptible to illness. During cold weather, limit time spent outdoors and be extremely cautious with any artificial sources of warmth such as heat lamps, as these can cause severe burns. Your old-timer may need a sweater to wear over his coat.

the balance of his life, then euthanasia is the right choice.

WHAT IS EUTHANASIA?

Euthanasia derives from the Greek, meaning *good death*. In other words, it means the planned, painless killing of a dog suffering from a painful, incurable condition, or who is so aged that he cannot walk, see, eat or control his excretory functions.

Euthanasia is usually accomplished by injection with an overdose of an anesthesia or barbiturate. Aside from the prick of the needle, the experience is usually painless.

MAKING THE DECISION

The decision to euthanize your dog is never easy. The days during which the dog becomes ill and the end occurs can be unusually stressful for you. If this is your first experience with the death of a loved one, you may need the

GERMAN SHORTHAIRED POINTER

The more openly you discuss the stressful occurrence of the aging and eventual loss of your pet, the easier it will be for you when the time comes.

comfort dictated by your religious beliefs. If you are the head of the family and have children, you should have involved them in the decision of putting your German Shorthaired Pointer to sleep. Usually your dog can be maintained on drugs for a few days in order to give you ample time to make a decision. During this time, talking with members of your family or even people who have lived through this same experience can ease the burden of your inevitable decision.

THE FINAL RESTING PLACE

Dogs can have some of the same privileges as humans. The remains of your beloved dog can be buried in a pet cemetery, which is generally expensive. If your dog has died at home, he can be buried in your yard in a place suitably marked with a stone or newly planted tree or bush. Alternatively, your dog can be cremated individually and the ashes returned to you. A less expensive option is mass cremation, although, of course, the ashes cannot then be returned.

There is usually a pet cemetery located in the vicinity of your home. Ask your vet to recommend a reputable cemetery.

A simple marker is a lovely tribute to a deceased pet.

Vets can usually arrange the cremation on your behalf. The cost of these options should always be discussed frankly and openly with your veterinarian.

GETTING ANOTHER DOG?

The grief of losing your beloved dog will be as lasting as the grief of losing a human friend or relative. In most cases, if your dog died of old age (if there is such a thing), he had slowed down considerably. Do you want a new German Shorthaired Pointer puppy to replace him? Or are you better off finding a more mature German Shorthaired Pointer, say two to three years of age, which will usually be housebroken and will have an already developed personality. In this case, you can find out if you like each other after a few hours of being together.

The decision is, of course, your own. Do you want another German Shorthaired Pointer or perhaps a different breed so as to avoid comparison with your beloved friend? Most people usually stay with the same breed because they know (and love) the characteristics of that breed. Then, too, they often know people who have the same breed and perhaps they are lucky enough that a breeder they know and respect expects a litter soon. What could be better?

SECOND-HAND POINTER

Some people choose to adopt or "rescue" an older dog instead of buying a new puppy. Some older dogs may have come from abusive environments and be fearful, while other dogs may have developed many bad habits; both situations can present challenges to their new owners. Training an older dog will take more time and patience, but persistence and an abundance of praise and love can transform a dog into a well-behaved, loyal companion.

GERMAN SHORTHAIRED POINTER

When you purchase your German Shorthaired Pointer, you will make it clear to the breeder if you hope to be buying a German Shorthaired Pointer with show prospects. No reputable breeder will sell you a young puppy and tell you that he is *definitely* of show quality, for so much can go wrong during the early months of a puppy's development. If you plan to show, what you will hopefully have acquired is a puppy with "show potential."

The first concept that the canine novice learns when watching a dog show is that each dog first competes against members of his own breed. Once the judge has selected the best member of each breed (Best of Breed), provided that the show is judged on a Group system, that chosen dog will compete with other dogs in his group. Finally, the dogs chosen first in each group will compete for Best in Show.

The second concept that you must understand is that the dogs are not actually compared against one another. The judge compares each dog against his breed standard, the written description of the ideal specimen that is approved by the American Kennel Club (AKC). Breeders attempt to get as close to this ideal as possible with every litter, but theoretically the "perfect" dog is so elusive that it is impossible.

If you are interested in exploring the world of dog showing, your best bet is to join your local breed club or the national parent club, which is the German Shorthaired Pointer Club of America. These clubs often host both regional and national specialties, shows only for GSPs, which can

MEET THE AKC

The American Kennel Club is the main governing body of the dog sport in the US. Founded in 1884, the AKC consists of 500 or more independent dog clubs plus about 4,500 affiliate clubs, all of which follow the AKC rules and regulations. Additionally, the AKC registers pure-bred dogs in the US and works to preserve the integrity of the sport and its continuation in the country. Over 1,000,000 dogs are registered each year, representing about 150 recognized breeds.

include conformation as well as obedience and field trials. Even if you have no intention of competing with your GSP, a specialty is like a festival for lovers of the breed who congregate to share their favorite topic: German Shorthaired Pointers! Clubs also send out newsletters, and some organize training days and seminars in order that people may learn more about their chosen breed. To locate the breed club closest to you, contact the American Kennel Club, which furnishes the rules and regulations for all of these events plus general dog registration and other basic requirements of dog ownership.

The American Kennel Club offers three kinds of conformation shows: an all-breed show (for all AKC-recognized breeds), a specialty show (for one breed only, usually sponsored by the parent club) and a Group show (for all breeds in the Group).

For a dog to become an AKC champion of record, the dog must accumulate 15 points at the shows from at least three different judges, including two "majors." A "major" is defined as a three-, four- or five-point win, and the number of points per win is determined on the number of dogs entered in the show on the day. Depending on the breed and its popularity, the number of points that are awarded varies. In more numerically strong breeds, more

dogs are needed to rack up the points.

At any dog show, only one dog and one bitch of each breed can win points. Dog showing does not offer "co-ed" classes. Dogs and bitches never compete against each other in the classes. Non-champion dogs are called "class dogs" because they compete in one of five classes. Dogs are entered in a particular class depending on their age and previous show wins. To begin, there is the Puppy Class (for 6- to 9-month-olds and for 9- to 12-month-olds); this class is followed by the Novice Class (for dogs that

Each dog, regardless of breed, is gaited around the ring so that the judge can evaluate movement.

have not won any first prizes except in the Puppy Class or three first prizes in the Novice Class and have not accumulated any points toward their champion title); the Bred-by-Exhibitor Class (for dogs handled by their breeders or handled by one of the breeder's immediate family); American-bred Class (for dogs bred in the USA!); and the Open Class (for any dog that is not a champion).

The judge at the show begins judging the Puppy Class, first dogs and then bitches, and proceeds through the classes. The judge places his winners first through fourth in each class. In the Winners Class, the first-place winners of each class compete with one another to determine Winners Dog and Winners Bitch. The judge also places a Reserve Winners Dog and Reserve Winners Bitch, which could be awarded the points in the case of a disqualification. The Winners Dog and Winners Bitch, the two that are awarded the points for the breed, then compete with any champions of record entered in the show. The judge reviews the Winners Dog, Winners Bitch and all the other champions to select his Best of Breed. The Best of Winners is selected between the Winners Dog and Winners Bitch. Were one of these two to be selected Best of Breed, it would automatically be named Best of Winners as well.

Finally the judge selects his Best of Opposite Sex to the Best of Breed winner.

At a Group show or all-breed show, the Best of Breed winners from each breed then compete against one another for Group One through Group Four. The judge compares each Best of Breed to his breed standard, and the dog that most closely lives up to the ideal for his breed is selected as Group One. Finally, all seven group winners (from the Sporting Group, Toy Group, Hound Group, etc.) compete for Best in Show.

To find out about dog shows in your area, you can subscribe to the American Kennel Club's monthly magazine, The *American Kennel Gazette* and the accompanying *Events Calendar*. You can also look in your local newspaper for advertisements for dog shows in your area or go on the Internet to the AKC's website, www.akc.org.

If your German Shorthaired Pointer is six months of age or older and registered with the AKC, you can enter him in a dog show where the breed is offered classes. Provided that your German Shorthaired Pointer does not have a disqualifying fault, he can compete. Only unaltered dogs can be entered in a dog show, so if you have spayed or neutered your GSP, you cannot compete in conformation shows. The reason for this is simple. Dog shows are the main forum to prove which

INFORMATION ON CLUBS
You can get information about dog shows from the national kennel clubs:

American Kennel Club
5580 Centerview Dr., Raleigh, NC 27606-3390
www.akc.org

United Kennel Club
100 E. Kilgore Road, Kalamazoo, MI 49002
www.ukcdogs.com

Canadian Kennel Club
89 Skyway Ave., Suite 100, Etobicoke, Ontario
M9W 6R4 Canada
www.ckc.ca

Fédération Cynologique Internationale
14, rue Leopold II, B-6530 Thuin, Belgium
www.fci.be

representatives of a breed are worthy of being bred. Only dogs that have achieved championships—the AKC "seal of approval" for quality in pure-bred dogs—should be bred. Altered dogs, however, can participate in other AKC events such as obedience trials and the Canine Good Citizen program.

Before you actually step into the ring, you would be well advised to sit back and observe the judge's ring procedure. The judge asks each handler to "stack" the dog, hopefully showing the dog off to his best advantage. The judge will observe the dog from a distance and from different angles, and approach the dog to check his teeth, overall structure, alertness and muscle tone, as well as consider how well the dog "conforms" to the standard. Most importantly, the judge will have the exhibitor move the dog around the ring in some pattern that he should specify. Finally, the judge will give the dog one last look before moving on to the next exhibitor.

If you are not in the top four in your class at your first show, do not be discouraged. Be patient and consistent, and you may eventually find yourself in a winning line-up. Remember that the winners were once in your shoes and have devoted many hours and much money to earn the placement. If you find that your dog is losing every time and never getting a nod, it may be time to consider a different dog sport or to just enjoy your GSP as a pet. Parent clubs offer other events, such as agility, tracking, obedience, instinct tests and more, which may be of interest to the owner of a well-trained German Shorthaired Pointer.

OBEDIENCE TRIALS

Obedience trials in the US trace back to the early 1930s when organized obedience training was developed to demonstrate how well dog and owner could work together. The pioneer of obedience trials is Mrs. Helen Whitehouse Walker, a Standard Poodle fancier, who designed a series of exercises after the Associated Sheep, Police Army Dog Society of Great Britain. Since the days of Mrs. Walker, obedience trials have grown by leaps and bounds, and today there are over 2,000 trials held in the US every year, with more than 100,000 dogs competing. Any registered AKC dog can enter an obedience trial, regardless of conformational disqualifications or neutering.

Obedience trials are divided into three levels of progressive difficulty. At the first level, the Novice,

dogs compete for the title Companion Dog (CD); at the intermediate level, the Open, dogs compete for the title Companion Dog Excellent (CDX); and at the advanced level, the Utility, dogs compete for the title Utility Dog (UD). Classes are sub-divided into "A" (for beginners) and "B" (for more experienced handlers). A perfect score at any level is 200, and a dog must score 170 or better to earn a "leg," of which three are needed to earn the title. To earn points, the dog must score more than 50% of the available points in each exercise; the possible points for each exercise range from 20 to 40.

Once a dog has earned the UD title, he can compete with other proven obedience dogs for the coveted title of Utility Dog Excellent (UDX), which requires that the dog win "legs" in ten shows. Utility Dogs who earn "legs" in Open B and Utility B earn points toward their Obedience Trial Champion (OTCh.) title. To become an OTCh., a dog needs to earn 100 points, which requires three first places in Open B and Utility under three different judges.

The Grand Prix of obedience trials, the AKC National Obedience Invitational gives qualifying Utility Dogs the chance to win the newest and highest title: National Obedience Champion (NOC). Only the top 25 ranked obedience dogs, plus any dog ranked in the top 3 in his breed, are allowed to compete.

MEETING THE IDEAL

The American Kennel Club defines a standard as: "A description of the ideal dog of each recognized breed, to serve as an ideal against which dogs are judged at shows." This "blueprint" is drawn up by the breed's recognized parent club, approved by a majority of its membership, and then submitted to the AKC for approval. The AKC states that "An understanding of any breed must begin with its standard. This applies to all dogs, not just those intended for showing."

AGILITY TRIALS

Having had its origins in the UK back in 1977, AKC agility had its official beginning in August 1994, when the first licensed agility trials were held. The AKC allows all registered breeds (including Miscellaneous Class breeds) to participate, providing the dog is 12 months of age or older. Agility is designed so that the handler demonstrates how well the dog can work at his side. The handler directs his dog over an obstacle course that includes jumps as well as tires, the dog walk, weave poles, pipe tunnels, collapsed tunnels, etc. While working their way through the course, the dog must keep one eye and ear on the handler and the rest of his body on the course. The handler gives verbal and hand signals to guide the dog through the course.

The first organization to promote agility trials in the US was the United States Dog Agility Association, Inc. (USDAA), which was established in 1986 and spawned numerous member clubs around the country. Both the USDAA and the AKC offer titles to winning dogs.

Agility is great fun for dog and owner with many rewards for everyone involved. Interested owners should join a training club that has obstacles and experienced agility handlers who can introduce

German Short-haired Pointers usually do well in trials that test their physical abilities, such as agility, shown here.

you and your dog to the "ropes" (and tires, tunnels, etc.).

FIELD TRIALS

Field trials are offered to the pointers, retrievers and spaniel breeds of the Sporting Group as well as to the Beagles, Dachshunds and Bassets of the Hound Group. The purpose of field trials is to demonstrate a dog's ability to perform his original purpose in the field. The events vary depending on the breed of dog, but, in all trials, dogs compete against one another for placement and for points toward their Field Champion (FC) titles.

The purpose of a field trial is

A handsome male GSP competing in a European show run by the Fédération Cynologique Internationale, the Continent's ruling dog organization.

for the dog to demonstrate the tasks in the field for which he was bred. Therefore, the tests for the pointing breeds differ from those designed for retrievers, spaniels, etc. The American Kennel Club holds Pointing Breed Field Trials, in which the German Shorthaired Pointer is eligible to participate. Aside from the GSP, the other breeds eligible for pointing breed competition are the Brittany, English Setter, German Wirehaired Pointer, Pointer, Gordon Setter, Irish Setter, Vizsla, Weimaraner and Wirehaired Pointing Griffon.

The AKC also holds an annual championship for the pointing breed gundogs. Dogs are judged on their all-around ability as gundogs, including skills in the field and how well they work with their handlers. This is not only an exciting competition for the dogs and their handlers but also a wonderful opportunity for spectators to see the pointing breeds in action, doing what they were meant to do!

HUNTING TESTS

AKC hunting tests evaluate a dog's skills in different areas of hunting. Tests include exercises with pointing, retrieving and flushing, all natural abilities of the German Shorthaired Pointer. As in obedience trials, each dog is scored against a set of points available for each exercise. Therefore, the dogs do not compete against each other, *per se*, but against themselves to earn as many points possible. The dog's ability to perform is judged against a standard of perfection established by the AKC Regulations; theoretically, every dog can be a winner!

Hunting titles offered by the AKC are Junior Hunter (JH), Senior Hunter (SH) and Master Hunter (MH). To earn a title, a dog must earn a qualifying score at the respective level. With each title comes a progression in difficulty. This is a wonderful opportunity for owners of German Shorthaired Pointers, whether or not they hunt regularly with their dogs. The breed's abilities in the field make them perfectly suited to training for and participating in hunting tests, and very capable of earning top titles.

TRACKING

Any dog is capable of tracking, using his nose to follow a trail. Tracking tests are exciting and competitive ways to test your German Shorthaired Pointer's natural scenting abilities. The AKC started tracking tests in 1937, when the first AKC-licensed test took place as part of the Utility level at an obedience trial. Ten years later in 1947, the AKC offered the first title, Tracking Dog (TD). It was not until 1980 that the AKC added the Tracking Dog Excellent title (TDX), which was followed by the Versatile Surface

JUNIOR SHOWMANSHIP
For budding dog handlers, ages 10 to 18 years, Junior Showmanship competitions are an excellent training ground for the next generation of dog professionals. Owning and caring for a dog are wonderful methods of teaching children responsibility, and Junior Showmanship builds upon that foundation. Juniors learn by grooming, handling and training their dogs, and the quality of junior's presentation of the dog (and himself) is evaluated by a licensed judge. The junior can enter with any registered AKC dog to compete, including an ILP, provided that the dog lives with him or a member of his family.

Tracking title (VST) in 1995. The title Champion Tracker (CT) is awarded to a dog who has earned all three titles.

In the beginning level of tracking, the owner follows the dog through a field on a long lead. To earn the TD title, the dog must follow a track laid by a human 30 to 120 minutes prior. The track is about 500 yards with up to 5 directional changes. The TDX requires that the dog follow a track that is 3 to 5 hours old over a course up to 1,000 yards with up to 7 directional changes. The VST requires that the dog follow a track up to five hours old through an urban setting.

INDEX

My German Shorthaired Pointer

PUT YOUR PUPPY'S FIRST PICTURE HERE

Dog's Name _____

Date _____ Photographer _____